CYMBALISMS

A COMPLETE GUIDE FOR THE ORCHESTRAL CYMBAL PLAYER

2 CDs INCLUDED

T0040766

BY FRANK EPSTEIN
CYMBALIST WITH THE BOSTON SYMPHONY ORCHESTRA

Edited by: Robert Sonner

ISBN 13: 978-0-6340-6329-9
ISBN 10: 0-6340-6329-4

HAL•LEONARD® CORPORATION
7777 W. BLUEMOUND RD. P.O. BOX 13819 MILWAUKEE, WI 53213

In Australia Contact:
Hal Leonard Australia Pty. Ltd.
4 Lentara Court
Cheltenham East, 3192 Victoria, Australia
Email: ausadmin@halleonard.com

Visit Hal Leonard Online at
www.halleonard.com

TABLE OF CONTENTS

ABOUT THE AUTHOR

A native of Amsterdam, Holland, percussionist Frank Epstein came to the United States in 1952, settling in Hollywood, California. Having joined the Boston Symphony Orchestra in 1968, he is now in his 39th season as percussionist with the orchestra. Mr. Epstein is a member of the faculty at the Tanglewood Music Center and the New England Conservatory, where he also founded and directs the NEC Percussion Ensemble and is Chairman of the Brass and Percussion Department. Mr. Epstein has made recordings with the Los Angeles Philharmonic, the Boston Symphony, the Boston Pops, and Collage New Music. As founder of Collage (and Music Director from its inception in 1972 through 1991), Mr. Epstein has overseen the commissioning and performance of over 200 new works written especially for the ensemble as well as the production of seventeen recordings. He has been involved with the Avedis Zildjian Company as a consultant on new product development (including the introduction of the Classic Orchestral Cymbal Selection), and as a clinician, conducting workshops and seminars throughout the United States, as well as Europe and Canada. Mr. Epstein holds a Bachelor of Music degree from the University of Southern California, Master of Music degree from New England Conservatory, and is also a graduate of the Tanglewood Music Center. His teachers included Robert Sonner, Earl Hatch, Murray Spivack, William Kraft, and Everett Firth. Before joining the Boston Symphony Orchestra he was a member of the San Antonio Symphony. Mr. Epstein was recently awarded a Presidential Commendation from the New England Conservatory for his work with Collage New Music.

ABOUT THE CD

All 104 excerpts on the accompanying CDs have been taken from Boston Symphony Orchestra broadcast tapes. In order to use these clips, special permission was received from the Boston local Union 9-535, the Boston Symphony Orchestra, and the BSO player's committee. The author is grateful for their cooperation in this matter. Pursuing and getting permission from the many conductors and soloists represented in these brief excerpts took a full three years. A book could be written on this process all by itself. However, I am pleased that in the end, permission was received from all involved. The availability of these excerpts should make for a complete understanding of the material covered in this book. In researching these excerpts and listening to multiple performances of each piece, I found that often my contribution, especially when the cymbal part is soft, can be difficult to hear. This is definitely not the case when one listens in the concert hall. It appears to be a matter of audio equipment as much as anything else. I hope the listener will still understand the musical gesture discussed by listening to, if not the precise cymbal sound, to the overall orchestra sound. In this way one can get a sense of what I am trying to project.

INTRODUCTION

Having been a member of the Boston Symphony for more than thirty-nine years, I can look back on a host of musical and magical moments, including moments of sheer beauty and excitement that transcend verbal description. Being a member of this great orchestra and having the luxury to perform in one of the great halls of the world has inspired me to develop my musical concepts. These concepts of sound, musicianship, precision, articulation, color, balance, and response occupy my every thought as it relates to the performance at hand.

In this treatise I will attempt to articulate as clearly as possible what I do and why. I include my thoughts on developing a good sound—a musical sound—which when all is said and done, is most crucial. Playing cymbals musically remains the ultimate challenge.

In order to facilitate my concepts, I have developed and formulated specific strokes. I have labeled these strokes "Cymbalisms," applying to cymbals a system in a similar manner in which the rudiments of snare drumming capture the essential elements of snare drumming. It is true that many of these strokes are relevant to the excellent instruments in my possession as well as to the fine hall in which I perform. However, I feel confident that others will want to incorporate them into their performance once they become aware of the possibilities of these techniques, the colors they produce, and the varied gestures that they amplify. It is my hope that, in time, others will develop additional techniques, and that a richer and more complete tradition of cymbal technique, including, "Cymbalisms," will be passed on from generation to generation.

ACKNOWLEDGMENTS

I would like to thank the members of my immediate family who have supported me: Margit Epstein and Peter Epstein. Their support over the many years has been a comfort and guiding light. Thank you to my wife, Mary Epstein, and my daughters Rebecca and Naomi, who continue to stimulate and challenge any and all of my precepts.

Thank you to Robert Sonner, my first percussion teacher, the editor of this endeavor, and my friend and colleague; Bill Grossman, for his computer expertise and help with printing of the repertoire excerpts; Russ Girsberger, New England Conservatory librarian, for his help in organizing the repertoire; Shawn Girsberger and Steven Emery for their expertise and skill as photographers; Brian Bell, producer, live concert broadcasts for WGBH radio, for his critical help in gathering the audio clips; Bridget Carr, BSO archivist, for her patient and efficient help in gathering audio source material; Patrick Keating, sound engineer at the New England Conservatory of Music for his expertise in producing the audio CD. Thanks also go to Lisa Nigris, head of the audio department at the New England Conservatory for her help and assistance in scheduling massive amounts of studio time; Karen Leopardi (assistant to the Boston Symphony Orchestra Music

Director) for her invaluable help and understanding in soliciting conductors and soloist clearance. A special thanks to all of my colleagues in the Boston Symphony, especially the gentlemen in my section whose professionalism and artistry continue to amaze me. Finally, I would like to thank the members of the Zildjian family for their support over the years, and a special thank you to the whole Zildjian team: Leon Chiappini, Lennie di Muzio (formerly with the Zildjian cymbal company), and Paul Francis.

Chapter One

CREATIVE INTERPRETATION OF THE ORCHESTRAL CYMBAL LITERATURE

Of all the various steps involved in playing cymbals, mental preparation is the most crucial. One must know the musical score and how cymbal notes affect or enhance the music. One must look at the score to understand how the notes fit into the overall texture and structure of the music. Further, during rehearsals, it is important to continuously listen musically, critically, and analytically. Some of the questions a player must answer are:

- What is the true nature of the notes?
- Is the cymbal part an integral part of the moment, or does it represent an added touch of color?
- Is the part important and soloistic, or is it part of the total mix?
- What is the nature of the musical gesture: is it ascending, descending, or linear?
- Should the cymbal notes dominate or should they be supportive?
- If the cymbal notes are supportive, what instruments are they supporting?

These and similar questions should *always* be in the mind of the cymbal player before making decisions about interpretation. If one determines that the cymbal part is dominant, either in a coloristic mode or for rhythmic purposes, the choice of cymbals becomes paramount.

General Directions:

The following directions represent cymbal choices and usage by the author that have proved successful in achieving the most satisfying and artistic results in playing some of the great orchestral repertoire.

> Throughout the musical examples in this book, single slashes (/) indicate when and where the cymbals are to be muted or cut off. A double slash (//) indicates a more aggressive cut off.

CYMBAL TONE

The cymbal sound is often important, and using the precisely correct cymbal becomes crucial. One must listen to the orchestra and prepare to match color, dynamics, and length of notes *at all times*. Matching cymbals to the overall dynamic and color mix of the music is also important. No matter how precisely a part is played, if the overall cymbal tone is too low or too high, it can sound absolutely wrong, an error akin to playing out of tune. Matching the orchestral color is crucial to enhancing and supporting the musical moment. Playing with high woodwind color or with low brass should trigger an immediate choice of cymbal that matches the color of these instruments.

Ravel's *Daphnis et Chloé* contains one of the most notable cymbal parts in the orchestral literature. It also highlights perfectly the above-mentioned concept of matching cymbal pitch (high and low) to the orchestral color. At measure 194, and for four measures after that, one could use a pair of 17" cymbals that produce a sound that is short and bright.

At measure 195, for just one measure, the mood changes rapidly and the tempo slows dramatically. Then, in the next measure, the *animè* resumes the preceding tempo, except that the orchestral pitch and orchestration is much deeper. Thus during this *lento* measure, change to 20" cymbals to produce a beautifully blended soft, short, and lower-pitched note.

🔊 **Ex. 1** *Daphnis et Chloé*, **Maurice Ravel**

CD 1 • Track 1   Conducted by Frubeck de Burgos on 4/7/05, Boston Symphony Orchestra

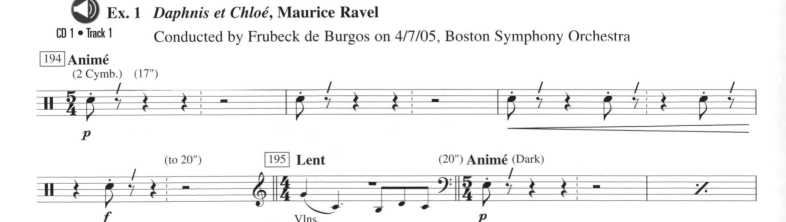

DYNAMICS

Equally important are the dynamic requirements of the moment. Some cymbals sound better *pianissimo*. Others sound better in the louder dynamics. In order to more accurately interpret the music, a quick switch of cymbals may become necessary, even though the part makes no mention of it. Dynamic and/or tonal contrast can more easily be affected by having another set of cymbals available.

In trying to answer the question, "What is the true nature of the notes?", one must consider whether the notes are active or passive. **Active** notes create energy, and **passive** notes dissipate energy. Active notes push sound through the air like lightning. Passive notes float like clouds. Active notes are often loud and short. Passive notes are usually soft and long. Active notes must be precisely measured as to length. Passive notes can often disappear or fade out on their own. Active and passive notes may occur in either crash cymbal or suspended cymbal parts. Some notes possess both active and passive qualities.

Most active notes that are played with crash cymbals are short in nature, and played in unison with the brass section. Most suspended cymbal notes are passive and coloristic in nature. However, there are a host of short suspended-cymbal notes in the repertoire in which active and rhythmic projection is the desired activity. Generally speaking, any suspended-cymbal part that includes a crescendo automatically should be considered as having an active function. Determining the exact function of cymbal notes is crucial to interpreting orchestral literature.

ATTACK AND ARTICULATION

Another important aspect is the nature of the attack or articulation. Cymbal notes can have a variety of attacks or beginnings, the same as with notes of all other instruments. However, specific articulations are rarely notated.

In developing a cymbal stroke, one must be able to vary the attack. Some notes must begin in a legato style, while others begin with an accent. Some must have an immediate and aggressive beginning, while others "sneak in." A stroke must be developed which can control the full spectrum of attacks needed. Playing a clean attack with no grace stroke or flam produces a legato stroke. Adding various grace notes can thicken or broaden the attack. It is not necessary that every crash-cymbal attack should sound like a "crash." Developing a smooth, legato stroke, resulting in a legato sound on crash cymbals should be everyone's immediate goal. Even in the loudest notes it is desirable to create a beautiful tone, with a beautiful attack, projecting volumes of cymbal sound without the result sounding like an explosion.

Likewise, by using two mallets, suspended cymbals can be controlled so as to produce a diversity of attacks. One should use a variety of mallets on different sizes of suspended cymbals in order to help produce the proper attack and most immediate sound. Whereas immediate cymbal sound is most desirable, limiting attack noise is just as important. By using two mallets, one on each side of the cup, there is more control over the cymbal. One can create more immediate sound, and can vary the attack by playing a variety of flam-type strokes. On suspended cymbals, unlike crash cymbals, the more legato that is called for, the wider the grace strokes. The more "attack," the closer together in time the two sticks should strike. Occasionally, the two mallets should play at the exact same moment, and the cymbal sound will just "pop" out. In certain instances, a player can use two different types of mallet to create just the right attack sound. The last note in the second movement of *La Mer* (Example 2), if played on suspended cymbals, could be just such an occasion.

Ex. 2: *La Mer, Mvt. 2*, **Claude Debussy (continued in Ex. 88)**

CD 1 • Track 2   Conducted by Robert Spano on 1/8/00, Boston Symphony Orchestra

MALLET PLACEMENT

The placement of the mallets on any particular cymbal is also an important factor. Assuming that a grace note will be played from left to right, placing the left mallet a bit closer to the cup and the right mallet on the extreme edge can help create the most sensitive and immediate of *pianissimo* strokes. In performing these "super-soft" notes, it is the grace notes that set the cymbal in motion. In the case of the *La Mer* excerpt, use of a softer mallet in the left hand for the grace note is recommended. This hides any contact noise while it sets the cymbal in motion in preparation for the main stroke by the right hand, which in this instance uses a slightly harder mallet.

The use of **cymbal hooks** (pictured right) to suspend cymbals can be very handy and effective. Cymbal hooks allow the cymbals to give out more sound, longer reverberation, and help minimize objectionable stick attack noise. Cymbal hooks do sometimes interfere with control of the cymbals, especially in fast, articulated passages. Nevertheless, the positive reasons far outweigh the negative, and thus cymbal hooks are heartily recommended.

CUT-OFFS

Determining the precise length of a note as well as the nature of the cut off is important. When cutting off a short note, one must be aware of the ambient acoustics. A cymbal sound, once in the air, is on its own. The nature of the moment and the acoustics at hand may very well affect when the note is to be stopped. Occasionally, in view of this percept, a note must be stopped a fraction of a second earlier. This idea becomes even more crucial if there is a *tutti* cut off for the entire orchestra. There is just such a place in Richard Strauss' *Don Juan*, (Example 3).

Ex. 3: *Don Juan*, **Richard Strauss**

CD 1 • Track 3   Conducted by Hans Graf on 8/16/98, Boston Symphony Orchestra

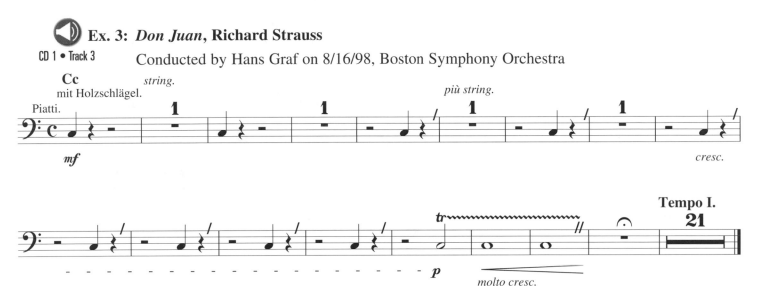

There is a *tutti* cut off just before the hold sign (//). The double slash indicates a hard, aggressive, and vigorous cut off. Acoustical consideration will help determine the precise moment when the cut off is to be made. In fact, the cut off inevitably should be made a moment before the general cut off, thereby helping to insure no possible overhang of cymbal sound.

Instruments such as cymbals, tam tams, and gongs typically must be dampened earlier than other instruments because of the danger of overhanging sound. Similarly, but perhaps more important, is the responsibility to play the notes and observe the rests as indicated. For a cymbal player, precisely observing the rests should be one of the most challenging activities. Knowing when to stop a note is as important as starting the note. Starting the note is in many ways easier.

Musical notation is generally very clear about when to play, but much less so about *when* to stop and *how* to stop a note. Typically a conductor's beat will help determine when to play, but few conductors indicate how and when to stop a cymbal note. The *how* and *when* questions are for me often the most interesting and challenging part of my performance. To study your own performances, listen to recorded playbacks in order to confirm whether or not you produced the most desirable length of a note. Ask a colleague whether a note sounded well playing *this* or *that* length. How a note is to be stopped—harshly, aggressively, gently, or very subtly—is related to what may be referred to as *musical gesture*; and it is difficult to notate. Often as not it is left to the performer's technical skills and musical taste to bring the proper musical gesture to fruition. Interpreting the music is the major objective of this book.

Chapter Two

EQUIPMENT

As important as the cymbals themselves is the need for a smoothly functioning cymbal holder. Cymbal holders are better than trays and tables in that the cymbals may be lifted in an upright position ready for play within a second. Trays and/or tables are important not only for storage of cymbals, but also for resting cymbals during a

performance or for cymbals not yet in play. Being able to put down the cymbals during measures of rest and be able to retrieve them immediately before playing is a notion strongly supported. An ideal setup is a combination of one or more cymbal holders, a table, and the availability of two or more suspended cymbal stands with hooks for attaching cymbals.

MATCHING CYMBALS

Having a number of good cymbals to play with is every percussionist's dream. The market is flooded with any number of cymbal manufacturers boasting the availability of good orchestral cymbals. However, close testing and scrutiny will determine fact from fiction. Quality orchestral cymbals are difficult to come by. Orchestral cymbals must be paired, matched, and mated. Finding one good cymbal is always possible. Finding the right match is more difficult.

Matching cymbals is a skill requiring time, patience, and experience. There are several factors to consider, one factor being "playability," which means that the cymbals must play well together. They must slide over one another without getting stuck, while at the same time allowing for full contact of one cymbal onto the other. When struck together, they must embellish and enhance one another. Especially when playing *pianissimo*, the cymbals must meet cleanly and slide apart effortlessly. Cymbals must be perfectly round, with the edging properly shaped so as to ensure a smooth contact at all times. When played at full dynamic levels, the sound of the two cymbals must match and blend. Yet the cymbals need not necessarily be tuned to the same pitch. Often the best pairing is one where one cymbal sounds just a half step or whole step apart from the other. The slight difference in pitch between the individual cymbals when played together will help create a more powerful mixing of sound. Often one cymbal will be slightly heavier than the other. This also helps to create a sound source rich in overtones, brilliance, and power.

SELECTION OF CYMBALS

Choosing two cymbals of proper weight and shape is important, for these factors determine and control pitch. The relative pitch that is projected by the two cymbals combined—selected in the manner previously described—will determine a good selection. The cymbals must provide the widest spectrum of sound, while at the same time projecting an overall sound mix which is neither too low nor too high in pitch. The symphony orchestra contains instruments of every size and shape. Consequently, the overall sound ambiance is rich and varied. The sound of an orchestra playing at full volume in a good hall remains one of the most exciting aural experiences known. Finding cymbals that fit into the orchestral texture and simultaneously are powerful enough to enhance the orchestral color is a challenge. Of course all the instruments in the orchestra do not play all the time at the same time. Cymbal parts are often written to be played with one orchestral section or another (woodwinds, strings, and/or brass). Cymbals must be found which blend well with these sectional orchestral colors.

CYMBALS NEEDED: SIZE

How many cymbals does one need? The real need is related to the size of the ensemble, the repertoire that is played, and the acoustics that surround the performance. A professional symphony orchestra of one hundred players, in one of the finer halls, must have a large selection of cymbals. First of all, there should be a basic, all-purpose set of 18" or 19" cymbals. In large concert halls, good 20" cymbals are recommended. These can be played both loudly and softly effectively. Small cymbals do not necessarily correspond to playing softer. Small cymbals often sound louder at soft dynamics because their sound source is higher and brighter; whereas a good pair of 19" or 20" cymbals—with a wider range of lower overtones or sound mix—can do the job much better.

A pair of 17" cymbals are good for playing fast and short notes, marches, stingers at the end of a piece, or fast repeated notes. These smaller cymbals are effective for color matching within the orchestral mix. Matching the color of the small cymbals in combination with the color of the larger cymbals for notes having the *same* dynamics within a piece is recommended. (See Example 1, Chapter One). Then again, use of the smaller cymbals for lighter moments in a piece is preferred where the sheer bulk and slower response of the larger cymbals would get in the way, whatever the dynamic might be. Some examples of music appropriate for the use the 17" cymbals include works by Rossini and other smaller, lighter pieces.

In the heavier repertoire (Tschaikowsky and Mahler), use of two sets of 18" cymbals in place of the 17" works well. The medium light 18" cymbals are used for quick, short strokes, and the medium heavy 18" for combination short and long strokes.

From personal experience, for many years, this author has used two sets of 20" cymbals to cover the bulk of the repertoire. The lighter of the two sets can be used to accentuate the softer dynamics, if these softer moments occurred most readily in the piece. Use the heavier pair if the dynamic pendulum swings the other way.

The largest cymbals—22" to 24"—are recommended for the heaviest kinds of play. 24" cymbals can be effective if used sparingly, perhaps once or twice in a loud piece for the two loudest and most dramatic moments. For the rest of the piece, 20" cymbals will work well. For the "Dancing Bear" scene of Stravinsky's *Petrouchka*, use of a combination of two very different size and weight cymbals can produce desirable results. In such a case, one could mount a somewhat heavy 18" cymbal on the bottom and a small 13" paper-thin cymbal on top. This combination allows for maximum control with most of the audible sound coming from the small cymbal.

Ex. 4 *Petrouchka* **(1947 version), Igor Stravinsky**

Conducted by Charles Dutoit on 8/24/04, Boston Symphony Orchestra

There is another special set of cymbals for Moussorgsky's *Pictures at an Exhibition*. I use a special set of 10" antique K cymbals for this piece. I have also used a modern set of 12" orchestral cymbals.

Ex. 5: *Pictures at an Exhibition, V. Ballet of the Unhatched Chicks*
Modeste Moussorgsky/Ravel (excerpt continued in Ex. 74)

Conducted by Charles Dutoit on 8/22/98, Boston Symphony Orchestra

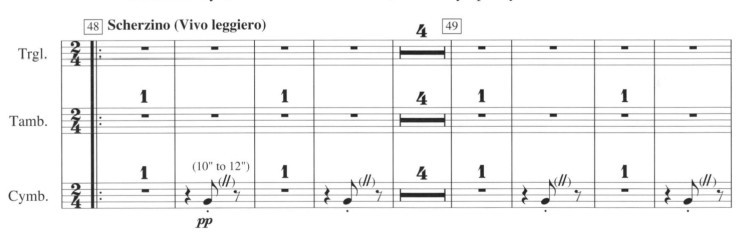

Some percussionists rely on at least a half-dozen suspended cymbals to satisfy all the possibilities encountered in the orchestral literature. Two or three of the cymbals may be each relegated to just one specific note in the entire repertoire, and are not used for anything else. This author has a special cymbal for the opening of the third movement of Debussy's *La Mer*. Though small in size (16"), this cymbal has a menacing quality just right for this section that depicts an upcoming storm.

In the next example, note that after the four cymbals strokes, a slightly larger and sweeter sounding suspended cymbal is called for, returning to the 16" cymbal one measure before rehearsal number **44**.

Ex. 6: *La Mer, Mvt. 3*, **Claude Debussy**

CD 1 • Track 6 Conducted by Robert Spano on 1/8/00, Boston Symphony Orchestra

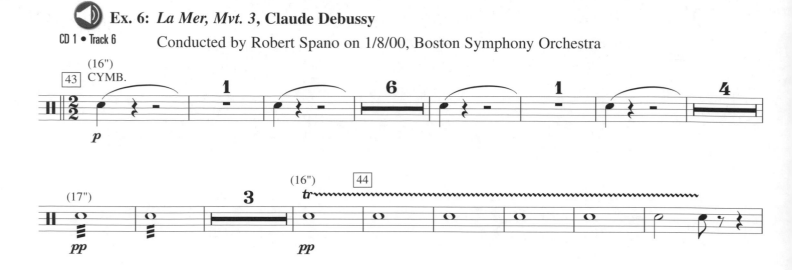

Another special example includes the opening of the fourth movement of Mahler's Symphony No. 1. Use of a powerful 18" cymbal struck with a heavy snare drum stick to produce the loudest and most immediate sound possible can create just the right sound.

Ex. 7: Symphony No. 1, Mvt. 4, Gustav Mahler

CD 1 • Track 7 Conducted by Jahja Ling on 1/5/04, Boston Symphony Orchestra

IV. Satz

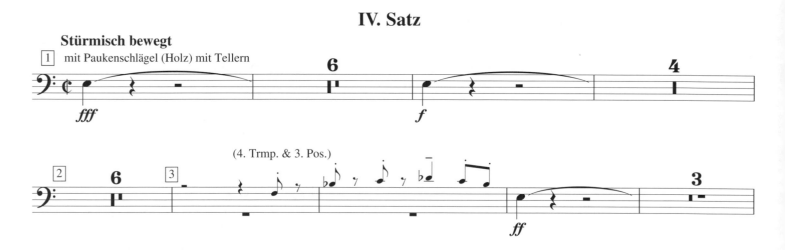

In general, suspended cymbals should be no larger than 18". The larger suspended cymbals can be unwieldy and unmanageable, as well as too low in pitch and too slow in response. Suspended cymbals must be quick and agile. Both crescendos and diminuendos must happen quickly and on demand. One must be able to control specific dynamics at every moment. A good 18" cymbal can be quick, powerful, and effective. A 17" cymbal can be used for quicker and lighter splashes. If more volume should become necessary, one can double-up and use two cymbals simultaneously. A player can roll on both cymbals using two mallets in each hand. Even better, on occasion, is to roll on one cymbal, and, at the top of the crescendo, strike a second cymbal together with the first, thereby insuring a solid and secure accent. Two 18" suspended cymbals can be effective in a piece like Prokofiev's *Romeo and Juliet*, as demonstrated in the next example.

Ex. 8: *Romeo and Juliet, Second Suite*, **Sergei Prokofiev**

CD 1 • Track 8   Conducted by Seiji Ozawa on 7/20/96, Boston Symphony Orchestra

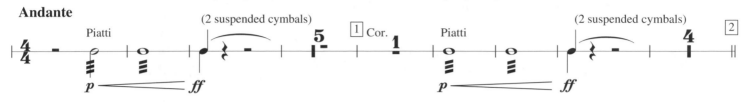

Similarly, a player may use two suspended cymbals simultaneously in a work such as Debussy's *La Mer*. As in the previous example, one could utilize one cymbal for the crescendo and land on two cymbals at the peak of the line. At rehearsal number **15** in Example 9, one cymbal for the eighth-note pick-up is used, landing on a second cymbal at the downbeat, thereby assuring a fresh, new and clean point of arrival. This technique is repeated at the next entrance. At the 2/4 measure, strike both cymbals forcefully, then cut them off rather quickly in preparation for the quarter rests that follow. Again, in the last measure, start the crescendo with one cymbal, and at the peak, stroke the second cymbal at the climax, immediately returning to the first cymbal to help control the diminuendo.

Ex. 9: *La Mer, Mvt. 1*, **Claude Debussy**

CD 1 • Track 9   Conducted by Robert Spano on 1/8/00, Boston Symphony Orchestra

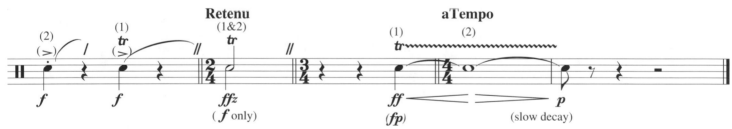

Near the dramatic ending of the piece, at number **61**, use two suspended cymbals simultaneously to help project the *ff*, return to a single cymbal for the *f*, and then return back to two cymbals for the next *ff*:

Ex. 10: *La Mer, Mvt. 3*, **Claude Debussy**

CD 1 • Track 10   Conducted by Robert Spano on 1/8/00, Boston Symphony Orchestra

CYMBAL MALLETS

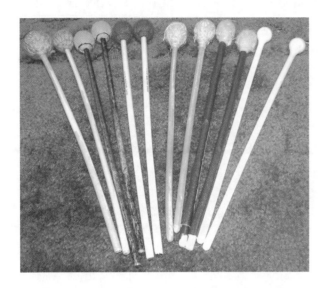

Along with a collection of cymbals, it may be useful to develop an array of cymbal mallets to help create the desired sounds a player imagines. These mallets should not be wound too tightly. As these mallets wear down, they should be rewound or replaced at frequent intervals. The material used for the winding should be wool.

The most important mallet to own is the general, all-purpose mallet, shown second from the far left in the above photo. The best way to describe this mallet is that it is similar to a medium-soft marimba mallet. This is the mallet of first choice and covers 80% of all cymbal play. It is the other 20% that requires some research and experimentation. Most of the repertoire can be covered with two distinctly different weight mallets. For example, a player could have one set that is utilized with most of the small suspended cymbals, and another set that gets used with most of the larger cymbals. For the smaller cymbals (16" and smaller), the mallets should be lighter in weight and wound slightly tighter. The mallets for the larger cymbals, 18" and larger, should also be larger, heavier, and more *loosely* wound.

Players may sometimes get into more extreme situations where a much harder or much softer set of mallets is desired. For the ending of Emmanuel Chabrier's *España*, the use of three white plastic bell mallets can be effective. In the ninth measure after letter **O** (see Example 12), prepare yourself by setting an inverted dustpan on a chair with your right foot on the dustpan, thus placing your knee directly under the suspended cymbal in preparation for the sixteenth notes that occur four measures from the end. The knee will allow you to balance the cymbal and mute it slightly at the same time. The mallets must strike the cymbal directly over the spot that is supported by the knee. All of the eighth notes before the measure of sixteenth notes should be played with the right hand that holds the two mallets. The other hand is used to muffle the cymbal.

In this case, striking the cymbals with two mallets allows for a more immediate response while the left hand is able to control and muffle each eighth note. The sixteenth-note passage is played with both hands (see photo: two mallets in the right and one in the left). The last two bars are struck with the right hand while the left hand muffles the isolated sixteenth note in each of these last two measures.

Ex. 12: *España*, Emmanuel Chabier

CD 1 • Track 12   Conducted by Keith Lockhart on 5/16/98, Boston Pops Orchestra

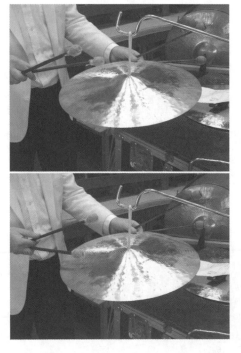

For the grace notes in Debussy's *La Mer*, at the fourth measure after rehearsal number **50**, a simple tactic is to use two suspended cymbals. Carry two very hard wound mallets in your right hand and two medium hard mallets in the left for the grace notes in the fourth measure. However, in preparation for the next three measures, drop the left-hand mallets onto the tabletop. Then with the left hand, prepare for the next entrance by muffling the suspended cymbal so that the following grace notes will be audible. Play the grace notes with your right hand (the one carrying two hard mallets) by rolling the wrist from the inside out so that two separate strokes are made. Muffling the cymbal is crucial to the success of this gesture.

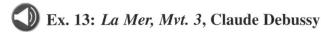

Ex. 13: *La Mer, Mvt. 3*, **Claude Debussy**

CD 1 • Track 13
Conducted by Robert Spano on 1/8/00, Boston Symphony Orchestra

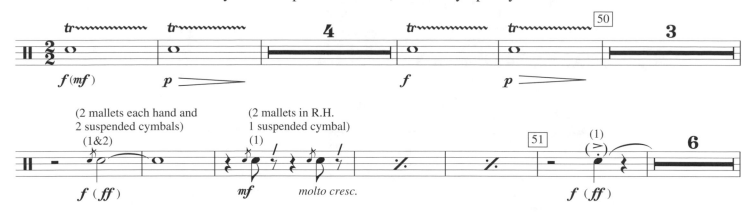

So far, four different pairs of mallets have been indicated. For the last note in Ravel's *Bolero*, use a 24" suspended cymbal. Because of the extreme size of this cymbal, use a mix of four mallets, two in each hand. Take both the regular pair of mallets and the softest pair of mallets, and place one of each in both hands, equidistant from the bell, and then *wail* away!

Ex. 14: *Bolero*, **Maurice Ravel**

CD 1 • Track 14
Conducted by Bernard Haitink on 4/22/96, Boston Symphony Orchestra

OTHER STICKS AND MALLETS

There is a need for a variety of snare drum sticks for playing on the different size and weight cymbals. Sticks include differently weighted shafts and differently sized and shaped beads that must be considered. Players should have a number of plastic and metal beaded sticks for more specialized sounds. A heavy pair of metal brushes is also necessary.

The normal drumset brushes typically are rendered inaudible in an orchestral situation. A heavier gauge metal wire should be used. The wire should be at least as thick as that of a typical coat hanger, yet made from a stiffer than ordinary metal. Several of these wires should individually be formed into the flat-fan shape with a handle, and covered with a metal sleeve or tube that is

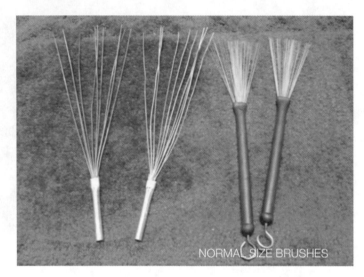

NORMAL SIZE BRUSHES

familiar to all of us. There are manufacturers today who offer a heavier brush design and it is worth it to seek them out.

Chapter Three

BASIC PLAYING POSITIONS

How and where one stands are equally important considerations. Your initial response, coming on stage, should be to position your cymbals, holder, and/or table, and music stand so that they are in an absolutely straight sight line with the conductor. Don't let anything interfere with this arrangement. If the stage is such that a small extension or adapter is needed in order for the cymbal setup to be perfectly positioned, insist on it. If it means asking the harp, piano, or celesta player to adjust their position slightly in order that your line of vision is unobstructed, negotiate that with them. Often you will have to negotiate for space with your most immediately neighboring colleagues. Getting enough room to swing unencumbered is crucial. Additional tables for storing extra cymbals also take more space. The best advice is to arrive early at rehearsals so that your physical set-up can be arranged well before the initial downbeat.

Once your cymbal setup and music stand are in position, place yourself behind them. Next, arrange your cymbal holder, any other instruments that are to be played, and your chair. *Where* one sits is important, too. If you place the chair directly behind the cymbals or music stand, eye contact and rapport with the conductor is lost. It is important to sit so you can easily see the conductor at all times, including the time one is not playing. You can thus quickly and efficiently stand up and get into position. Often it is important to make final adjustments in relation to other colleagues in the percussion section to assure that there is enough space side-to-side and front-to-back, in order to comfortably do the job.

FOOT POSITION AND STANCE

Before preparing to play, make sure that, when standing, you are comfortable with your surroundings.  *Everything* must be in order: stand, music, cymbals, suspended cymbals, and mallets. Often split-second timing is required when changing cymbals, or dropping or picking up mallets within a measure. When you stand, spread your legs apart, with one leg slightly ahead of the other, placing your weight squarely on both legs. Try to keep your body, both legs, arms, and back, loose and resilient

so as to facilitate whatever strokes are to be made. Being able to shift weight from one leg to another is important, for in cases when a full stroke is made, the weight shifts from front to back.

GRIP

The importance of the cymbal **grip**—how one actually holds the cymbals—is a step often overlooked. First of all it is important to keep the cymbal straps in good condition. The straps must be flat and neat. If the straps are allowed to be twisted and curled, the hard edges can dig into the fingers and cause pain and discomfort.

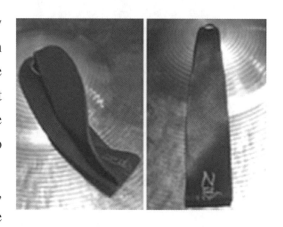

Take the straps and place them in your hand, between the first finger and thumb, putting the thumb on top. This next consideration is most important: be sure that there is approximately a half-inch of space between the thumbs and the cymbals. Do not attempt to grab the cymbal as tightly as possible, nor as close to the cymbal cup as possible. The space

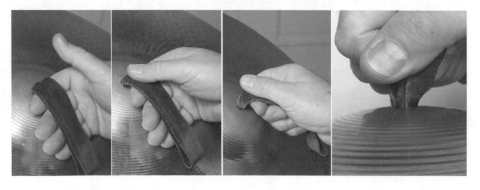

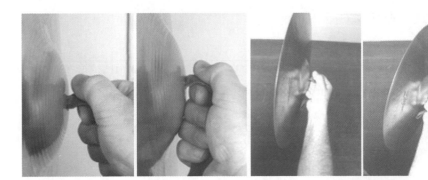

between the thumb and cymbal is necessary for the cymbal to vibrate properly. A player can achieve the proper control by rotating the hands and forearms together, thereby positioning both cymbals in a vertical manner. When both cymbals are held exactly perpendicular to the floor and about one inch apart, one is in "playing position." Apply only a minimum amount of thumb pressure on the straps, and use the arm muscles and wrist rotation to keep them there.

THE BASIC STROKE

The path of the stroke is somewhat like an inverted teardrop shape. Immediately after contact is made, the right cymbal continues its movement downward, creating a momentary slide, before moving away from the cymbal and eventually moving upward into position for the next note.

This stroke is made with the *right cymbal only*, up to a *mezzo forte* dynamic level. The left cymbal first reacts by moving *out* when struck, and then *back* into position *immediately* after. As the demand for louder dynamics increases to *forte* or more, the left cymbal begins its own cycle that is exactly opposite to the right cymbal. For me, the most important consideration is that, at the moment of impact, both cymbals should meet "in round" as much as possible. That is, at the moment of impact, the *entire* right cymbal should meet

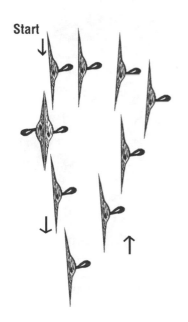

the *entire* left cymbal at the same time. Quality of sound is determined by the success of this meeting "in round." For the cymbals to meet "out of round" is to sacrifice a full and beautiful sound.

Many players prefer to have their cymbals meet up to an inch or more "out of round." This is definitely easier and requires less skill, but the effect is that the sound becomes somewhat washed out and distorted because the cymbals set up an abbreviated vibration series, resulting in a weaker sound.

ELEVEN BASIC STEPS

Because cymbal sounds should not hang over into orchestral silences or notated rests, all of your stroking should be downward, with the ability to muffle and/or choke notes into the chest area as quickly as is necessary. Where cymbal notes are intended to ring on, you will be able to continue onward into the air. The stroke is based on developing a clean and consistent sound, maximum tone, minimum impact noise, and a fluent follow-through. The strokes should be consistent with your conviction that cymbal notes have a specific duration and that notes should be stopped when either the notation or the music demands it. For these concepts to be achieved, the following steps are recommended. Each one, when mastered in order, will lead to a successful cymbal stroke.

1: The Hi-hat "Chick" Stroke

Hold the left cymbal still, and perpendicular to the floor. It must also be parallel to and at the same height as the right cymbal. The left cymbal does not move.

The right cymbal— also perpendicular to the floor and absolutely parallel to the left cymbal—should be brought into contact with the other cymbal so that both cymbals meet perfectly "in round." *All* of one cymbal should make contact with the *entire* other cymbal at the same instant. The sound created is not allowed to ring. This is accomplished by pushing the cymbals together. The sound is cut short and a resulting "chick" sound is heard. Repeat this movement many times. Check by looking in a mirror to see that the cymbals are perfectly "in round" at the moment contact is made. Play at one stroke per beat, and repeat until *mm* ♩ = 52. Once this first step is accomplished, the cymbals should meet perfectly aligned every time. The entire surface of the right cymbal should meet the entire surface of the left cymbal at the same time: no flam, no grace note, no "bubble."

2: The Sizzle Stroke

Step 2 requires you to relax the horizontal pressure just a bit, immediately after contact is made. It begins at the moment that the cymbals are in contact. Relaxing some of the horizontal pressure allows the cymbals to vibrate against one another for just an instant. The resulting sound is like that of a sizzle cymbal being struck with one's finger. Facility in perfecting this exercise—in fact *all* of these exercises—can be helped immensely by practicing the strokes with the eyes closed. This forces you to trust your ears and react accordingly.

3: The Slide Stroke

With Steps 1 and 2 accomplished, a "mini-slide" can be added to the *Sizzle*. The concept of the slide is basically that contact between the cymbals is of a specific duration. The exact duration of this slide is controlled by the player and may be increased or decreased depending on the particular sound desired. Unfortunately, many players, once they achieve this slide stroke, tend to overdo it, thereby spoiling the effect of this very subtle stroke. The slide portion of the stroke in a normal crash is of a momentary nature, enriching and broadening the contact of the two cymbals while simultaneously distilling the impact noise otherwise created. However, care must be taken not to overdo this part of the stroke.

The goal here is to slide the right cymbal downward against the left cymbal with enough pressure to keep the cymbals in contact but with not too much pressure to inhibit the sizzle effect created in Step 2. The slide

should only be an inch or a bit more in length. The follow-through motion that immediately follows contact is a most critical part of the stroke, and when it is done correctly, it will help guarantee a beautiful sound. This final part of the stroke will also minimize contact noise and minimize air pockets. Repeat until you achieve $\quarternote = 52$.

4: The Pianissimo Stroke

All of the stroking thus far has been done in a slow but even pace at a tempo of about ♩ = 52. By gently, slowly, and steadily speeding up the stroke, starting from ♩ = 52, and not allowing for any other changes in sound, pressure, or contact, a "pianissimo stroke" should result. The left cymbal should be stationary. The distance between the two cymbals is no more than one inch and decreases as the speed of the stroke increases. Contact is made evenly, and the cymbals remain in perfect round at the moment of contact. The

length of the "slide" in Step 3 is now reduced from one inch to just a quarter of an inch. The sound of this stroke should result in a beautiful *pianissimo* stroke, relaxed and consistent every time. If one practices these exercises, and particularly this one, with the eyes closed, it will facilitate the growth of the skills in a dramatic way! In this instance, increase the speed until achieving ♩ = 92.

5: The Pianissimo Stroke Refined

Step 5 is designed to help control the *pianissimo* stroke further and to allow more practice stroking in a slower tempo. The idea here is to slow down our stroking from ♩ = 92 to ♩ = 20. As we slow down, and more time is created between the strokes, the cymbals may become more difficult to control. Keep the slide short (about a quarter of an inch or less). If the cymbal becomes difficult to control, speed up the stroke once in awhile to regain control. Once again, it is important to practice such an exercise with your eyes closed. It will increase your sensitivity to the kinesthetic aspects. With mastery of this step, hopefully you should become able to make a perfect *pianissimo* stroke the very first time and every time thereafter, if the passage calls for it.

6: The Mezzo-forte Stroke

It is important to remind you that throughout Steps 1 through 6, the left cymbal is stationary. Thus far all strokes presented have employed the softer dynamics. Learning to play cymbals can otherwise be a noisy affair, but with this approach, our hearing will not be damaged at the outset. We need to listen carefully to the sounds being produced—tone, attack, and color—to help insure consistent sounds as we go on. Getting a bit louder is not a problem. We simply speed up the stroke and increase the distance between the cymbals

before the stroke is made. For Step 6, no other changes are necessary. Increase the distance between the two cymbals to one inch, then two, and then three, keeping in mind not to involve the stationary left cymbal. The overall sound should remain consistent yet louder as the cymbals move farther apart. Work gradually up to ♩ = 52.

7: The Forte Stroke

In order to get to a *forte* level, the left cymbal must now come into play. Initially, as the distance increases between the two cymbals, and the left cymbal absorbs more and

more of the initial shock, it must react. In Step 7, this reaction takes the form of a gentle swaying movement back and forth away from the initial blow and then back into position.

The right cymbal should execute the same motion as it had when stroking at the softer level. The approach thus far has been almost direct. Now, as we increase the distance between the two cymbals, the right cymbal should start up a bit higher, coming over the left and into it. Meanwhile, the left cymbal—in preparation for the moment of contact—should tilt slightly away from the right cymbal. One should not choke up on the straps, but stay relaxed and simply allow the left cymbal to move back and forth. This will allow a *forte* stroke with the same consistency of sound and the same initial attack (clean and *legato* in nature) as the initial sounds made in the earlier steps. Repeat until achieving ♩ = 100.

Sergei Prokofiev, in his *Scythian Suite*, incorporates an unusual cymbal part written for two players, each playing a suspended cymbal, thus taking this idea to another level. This loud and aggressive—if not barbaric—music is seldom performed.

 Ex. 11: *Scythian Suite*, **Sergei Prokofiev**

Conducted by Gennady Rozhdestvensky on 1/20/01, Boston Symphony Orchestra

In the case of the author's personal cymbal collection, the total number of pairs of cymbals include: one pair of medium-heavy 16", one pair of medium 17", two pairs of 18" (medium-light and medium-heavy), two pairs of 20" (medium-light and medium-heavy), one pair of 22", and one pair of 24" crash cymbals. In addition, a special pair of 14" cymbals are included for use exclusively for Beethoven's Ninth Symphony, as well as a

12 *Chapter Two:* Equipment

8: The Fortissimo Stroke

For cymbal strokes beyond the *forte* level, the left hand must become more and more active. The reflex motion set up in Step 7 evolves in Step 8 into a full up-and-down motion, exactly opposite to the motion of the right cymbal, which is down-and-up. As the distance between the cymbals increases, and as the two cymbals are put into motion, the increased impact of the blow is absorbed by the moving left cymbal. Consistent, beautiful, loud cymbal strokes will be achieved.

It may be helpful to start all cymbal strokes, especially the louder strokes, from the same starting position: both cymbals parallel to each other, an inch apart and perpendicular to the floor. This allows for a momentary reference point before opening up the distance between the cymbals, raising the right cymbal up and lowering the left cymbal down. This preparatory movement is precisely timed with the conductor's upbeat. As he/she moves the baton toward the downbeat, you should in turn, move the cymbals along at the exact same rate, and meet him/her at the right moment. Another important ingredient in making a beautiful loud stroke is to adjust the distance between the cymbal cup and the hand. The louder the stroke, the more you should move back on the strap, away from the cup. This allows the cymbals maximum flexibility when they meet, and maximum freedom during the rest of the stroke. Repeat this until achieving ♩ = 80.

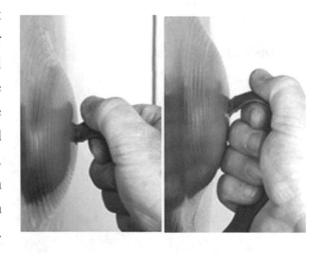

The following sequence of photographs shows the complete range of physical action that accompanies a *fortissimo* cymbal crash. Take special note of the follow-through, described more fully in Step 10.

9: The Flam Stroke

The size of the flam is determined by the angle of the right cymbal. The use of a flam or grace stroke is somewhat inevitable and often desirable, especially in the louder strokes. However, the size of the grace stroke is controllable by the angle of the right cymbal. The more *legato* the sound desired, the more important the angle of the right cymbal becomes. The louder the stroke, the larger the flam used. Remember to loosen up on the grip (especially on the left cymbal) so that, at the moment the right cymbal begins to meet the left cymbal, the left cymbal is free enough to respond and mesh, and to receive the forthcoming blow delivered by the remainder of the right cymbal. This increased relaxation and flexibility of the cymbals will absorb some of the attack and help insure a more beautiful loud stroke. Should one want to create a loud stroke with more attack sound (less tone), the left cymbal should be held more rigid, and a stronger attack will ensue.

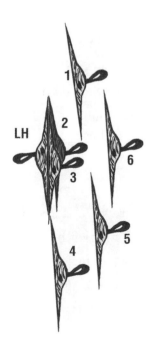

10: Follow-through

The follow-through is one of the more interesting aspects of cymbal performance. The follow-through itself, as well as the path it takes, where it stops, how fast it travels, and what happens after the cymbals stop moving, all lend to interpretation of the quality of the musical gesture one is trying to portray. For the longest and most exclamatory notes, try to keep the cymbals in motion in direct relation to how long you want the cymbals to remain "active." In certain cases, try to bring both cymbals up over your shoulders, where they can then settle down into a passive position. Other notes may be cut off before they reach any height at all.

The vigor that one uses to cut off the sound also indicates something about the character of the note. Cymbals in motion add drama, energy, and intensity. Cymbals allowed to stop in mid-air dissipate energy and bring the sound to a gentle stop.

11: The Cutoff

Cutting cymbals off, or stopping the sound, is also an integral aspect of performance. Cymbals may be stopped in the chest area. Depending on what one's body type is, it may be easier or more efficient to pull the cymbals onto the upper part of the stomach. This somewhat softer surface will often produce a more complete and immediate cutoff. In order to protect the chest area, faster and louder cutoffs should be done at or near the upper part of the stomach, while **slower cutoffs are better done at chest level.**

Sometimes when the cutoff is vigorous and done during the active part of the sound, one can add another exciting dimension to the performance. Actually, there are two possibilities here. One can make a crash, leaving the cymbals pretty much in place and making a vigorous cutoff. Or one can directly cut the cymbals while moving them about and into the chest. The two methods are distinctly different. For the most precise and rhythmic performance, leaving the cymbals in place is more accurate.

However, cutting them off while the cymbals are in motion is infinitely more exciting! On occasion, the cutoff is done slowly, so as not to disturb the concluding cymbal vibrations or the musical moment at hand. In fact, *all* cymbal performance involves the cutoff, and so careful consideration must be given to how and when the cutoff should occur.

Chapter Four

BASIC ORCHESTRAL REPERTOIRE

The limitation of musical notation in interpreting orchestral repertoire is such that personal preference, musical taste, and technique often override what is printed on the page. Musical notation tells a player relatively little, especially when it comes to percussion parts. Basic questions need to be answered. For example, what is the real length of the note? And, what is the quality of the musical gesture? Or, what is the function of the percussion during any one particular episode? Many people automatically assume the function of the cymbal player is to add color to the orchestra. In fact, the cymbal player must provide a solid rhythmic foundation, often in unison with the bass drum, and usually with the brass section.

MUSICAL NOTES: ACTIVE, PASSIVE, AND SILENCE

Any musical note has two basic attributes: active and passive. The **active** mode includes the beginning of the note through the point where it becomes passive. Because of the natural decay of cymbal sound, the active mode is further enhanced through movement of the cymbal in the air. So, as long as the cymbals are in motion, they are active, and the sound is being projected outward. The **passive** mode of the sound can be dealt with in one of two distinct ways. One can stop moving the cymbals in mid-air and let them dissipate further in a natural way, or the sound can be gently stopped at any time during the passive mode. In stopping the sound during the active mode while the cymbals are in motion, one can forcefully create the "sound" of silence, a powerful tool in music making. It often takes as much energy to cut off the sound during the active mode as it does to create the sound in the first place. One can also sustain the cymbal sound in its passive mode and then cut off the remaining sound. In this case there are three parts to the sound: active, passive, and silence.

Let us look at a few examples. The first two feature the cymbals in a unique way. The music and its orchestration serve to enhance the sound of the cymbals. In short, one can't go wrong. It is perfect writing for cymbals...that is, except for the notation!

Consider note length first. There are numerous examples of quarter notes and eighth notes in the literature where it is commonly agreed that it would be ludicrous to play what is actually written in the part. The opening of the fourth movement of Symphony No. 4 by Tschaikowsky is perhaps the most well-known example of this problematic anomaly. The question remains, how long is this note? The opening cymbal note is written as an eighth note. However, the note played by the rest of the orchestra is a half note followed by a dotted quarter note and then an eighth note. It is clear that the active mode of this note should last for a half note, the passive mode should last for a dotted quarter, and the eighth note suggests a cutoff. The overall character of this note is one of energy and exuberance.

 Ex. 15: Symphony No. 4, Mvt. 4, Peter I. Tschaikowsky

CD 1 • Track 15   Conducted by Bernard Haitink on 1/31/98, Boston Symphony Orchestra

Allegro con fuoco

The quarter note in the first measure of Example 16 should in fact be held for three full measures! The music referred to is Georges Bizet's *Carmen Suite No. 1, No. 5, Les Toreadors*. Here in the opening measures there is an additional problem of interpretation. The notation is clearly wrong! The proper sound here is to let the cymbal ring throughout the measure and into the next—there is no passive mode. All is active, and the sound is stopped at the last possible moment only to recover to make the next entrance as cleanly as possible. The characteristics of this note are excitement, brilliance, and majesty.

However, four measures before rehearsal letter **A**, the quarter note should be played as a true quarter note. Play the next measure in the same way, and two measures before letter **A**, the eighth notes become true eighth notes. Then again at letter **A**, the soft, stroked half notes play through the next measures. Listen to the music!

Ex. 16: *Carmen Suite No. 1, No. 5, Les Toreadors*, **Georges Bizet**
Conducted by David Allan Miller on 5/28/94, Boston Pops Orchestra

Allegro giocoso. (♩ = 116)

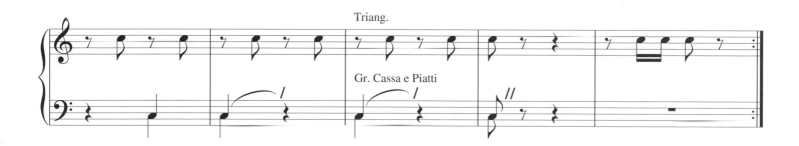

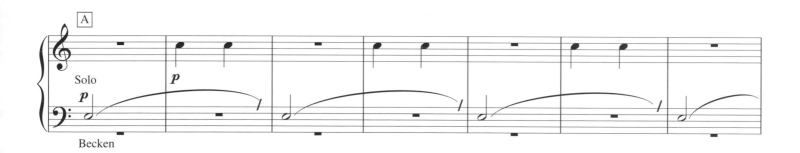

La Valse, by Maurice Ravel, provides us with another example of exceptional orchestral writing. The cymbal sound is glorious no matter what one does. However, the discriminating cymbal player must take note: every half note should be played exactly as written. All the rests must be strictly adhered to and the cymbal sound is cut off, except the last one. The last half note before rehearsal number **18** should sound through to the next measure.

Ex. 17: *La Valse*, **Maurice Ravel**

Conducted by Seiji Ozawa on 12/6/97, Boston Symphony Orchestra

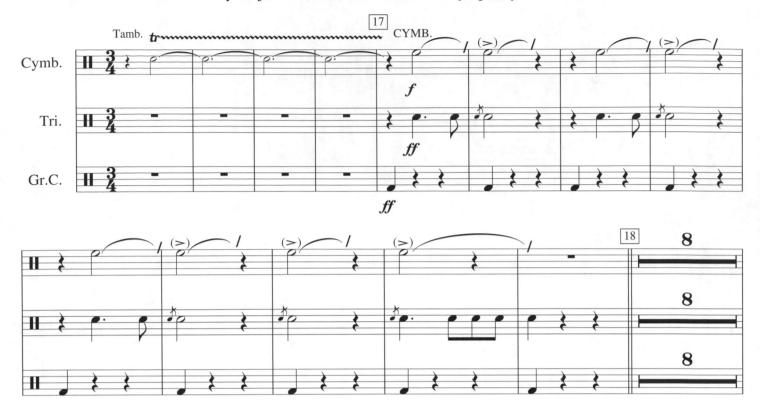

COMPOSERS

The remainder of this chapter is dedicated to specific examples in the orchestral repertoire by some of its most notable composers. In some cases, multiple works are represented from a composer in an attempt to demonstrate their style in writing for cymbals across a larger sampling of compositions.

PETER I. TSCHAIKOWSKY

There is a wealth of repertoire in which composers' intentions are very clearly indicated. Personal preference should not be abused when dealing with this repertoire. Some of these works include most of the repertoire of Tschaikowsky, including examples from the fourth movement of Symphony No. 4, *Romeo and Juliet Overture*, the *1812 Overture*, *Capriccio Italien*, and *Swan Lake*.

In Symphony No. 4, beginning at twelve measures before number **13** (Example 18), there are six measures that never fail to give the cymbal player a banging headache. These six innocent-appearing measures—though technically easy to play—are musically very difficult to coordinate. The second and fourth beats in the first three measures are played together with the full brass. However, starting in the fourth measure, the cymbal player and the entire rest of the orchestra part company.

Ex. 18: Symphony No. 4, Mvt. 4, Peter I. Tschaikowsky

Conducted by Christoph von Dohnanyi on 7/7/04, Boston Symphony Orchestra

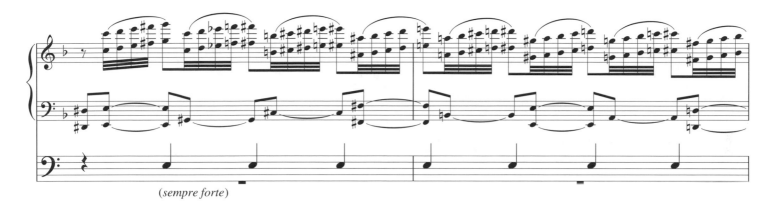

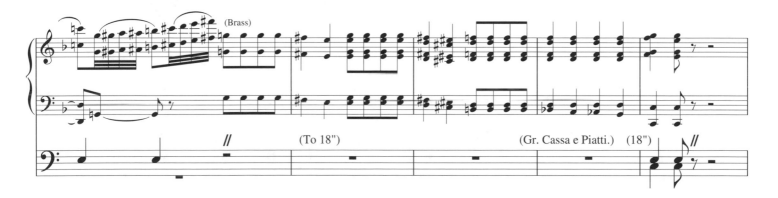

The full orchestra begins an offbeat pattern in which the strong beats are on the after-beats, while the cymbal player must stay on the weaker downbeats. Typically, conductors who tend to favor the majority and thus stress the offbeat pattern (making the cymbal player's already difficult role even more difficult), further aggravate the situation. Suggestion: focus on the pulse, and maintain a steady beat. And because it takes a moment to initiate the offbeat pattern during the first beat of the fourth measure, it sometimes requires a brief hesitation before playing the second, third, and fourth beats. In this example, remember: if it sounds right, you are wrong!

Let's take a closer look at the end of the fourth movement of Tschaikowsky's Symphony No. 4. Depending on the tempo, the ending of movement is either a cymbalist's dream or a nightmare. At the very least it remains a challenge.

For the first measure, play the notes exactly as written. In the second and third measures, let the cymbals ring through for two beats and cut them off sharply. The remainder of the movement should be played as accurately as possible, including obeying the rests!

Ex. 19: Symphony No. 4, Mvt. 4, Peter I. Tschaikowsky (see stroke #16, Chapter 5)

CD 1 • Track 19   Conducted by Christoph von Dohnanyi on 7/7/04, Boston Symphony Orchestra

There is one exception, and it is in the first and second measure of number **13** (Example 20). In this measure, let the eighth notes ring through despite the notation and despite the fact that this is a rhythmic passage. The reason for this exception is found in the score. The notation for the cymbal part is opposite of, yet equal to the brass part. In these two measures the cymbals are the only instruments in the orchestra playing offbeats, while the brass play full downbeat quarter notes. The eighth notes in these two measures will sound better ringing through, as they would draw excessive attention to the cymbal part if they were cut off as the notation indicates.

 Ex. 20: Symphony No. 4, Mvt. 4, Peter I. Tschaikowsky

CD 1 • Track 20   Conducted by Christoph von Dohnanyi on 7/7/04, Boston Symphony Orchestra

Afterward, however, each should be cut off sharply so as to accentuate the eighth- and quarter-note rests as indicated. This takes the theory to the extreme, but it works well and helps keep the cymbal sound out of the rests, making for a more unified overall sound. Some phrase accents have been added to help support the musical line. Additionally, the inclusion of "tutti play" needs some explanation. **Tutti play** is when the bass drum and cymbals exactly double the overall rhythm of the orchestra. This usually also involves doubling the brass section. During this kind of play, it is wise to always underplay the dynamic, thereby assuring the cleanest kind of play.

In all of these excerpts there are significant sections in which the cymbal part simply supports the overall rhythm (*tutti* play). In strict unison *tutti* passages like these, the cymbal player must play not only the notes, but the rests as well. It does not make sense for the entire orchestra to project specific rhythms and have the cymbal player ringing through the rests. In every one of these cases, the cymbal sound should be stopped during its active mode.

Similar thinking is applied to the other "chestnut" of the cymbal repertoire, Tschaikowsky's *Romeo and Juliet Overture Fantasy* (Example 21). This famous excerpt—found on most percussion auditions—requires two sets of cymbals. The eighth notes are to be played cleanly, but not as short as possible, and should be played with 18" cymbals. During the two-measure rest preceding the half note passage (measures 6 and 7 after **E**), change to 20" cymbals. The half notes should be allowed to ring for two beats, and then cut off sharply at the bar line. However, for the third bar of half notes, make allowance for the quick short eighth note that follows. Depending on the tempo, first try to cut this note off as well. If the tempo is too fast, then try for a "half-cut" and choke only the left cymbal while allowing the right to prepare for the short note to follow. If this fails to do the job, let the half note ring through the eighth rest and then play the short note.

 Ex. 21: *Romeo and Juliet Overture*, **Peter I. Tschaikowsky**

CD 1 • Track 21   Conducted by Seiji Ozawa on 7/25/99, Boston Symphony Orchestra

Another excerpt from this piece also calls for some critical cutoffs (Example 22). Play this section with 18" cymbals. Every note—the quarter notes and the eighth notes—should be played exactly as written. The rests should be strictly observed, in keeping with the sense of true *tutti* play, except for the very last note at ten measures after **T**. This note tends to be elongated by the whole orchestra and ends up being more or less a quarter note that is abruptly stopped, allowing for a clean fourth-beat rest. Underplay much of the eighth-note passage and try to make a considerable crescendo in the last three measures leading into the final measure.

 Ex. 22: *Romeo and Juliet Overture*, **Peter I. Tschaikowsky**

CD 1 • Track 22   Conducted by Seiji Ozawa on 7/25/99, Boston Symphony Orchestra

In the following three excerpts, each note is played exactly as written and all the rests are strictly observed. However, Examples 23, 24, and 25 offer exceptions to the so-called *tutti* rule. The notes with slur markings are allowed to ring through for purely musical reasons.

Ex. 23: *1812 Overture*, **Peter I. Tschaikowsky**

CD 1 • Track 23
Conducted by Keith Lockhart on 5/18/99, Boston Pops Orchestra

Ex. 24: *Capriccio Italien*, **Peter I. Tschaikowsky**

CD 1 • Track 24
Conducted by John Williams on 8/2/96, Boston Symphony Orchestra

Più presto.

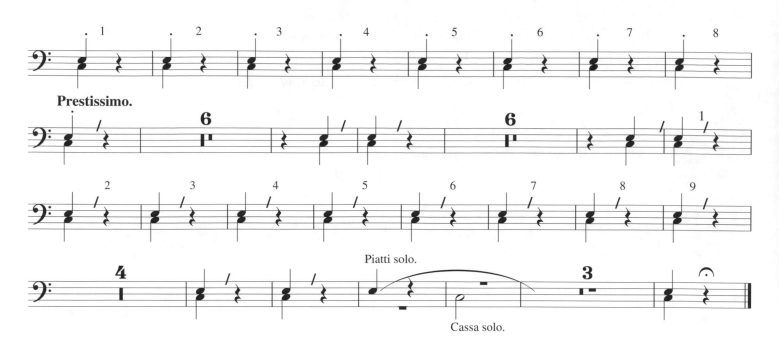

Prestissimo.

Ex. 25: *Swan Lake, No. 5, Danse Hongroise, Czardas*, **Peter I. Tschaikowsky**

CD 1 • Track 25 — Conducted by Seiji Ozawa on 11/18/78, Boston Symphony Orchestra

Piatti solo.

Cassa solo.

NICOLAI RIMSKY-KORSAKOV

A discussion of *Scheherazade*, by Rimsky-Korsakov (Example 26), is not complete without mentioning the special problems created by the composer. For the first ten measures of Example 26, one is playing on crash cymbals. However, during the next seven measures of rest, one must change to suspended cymbals. Set up two suspended cymbals in order to prepare for the sixteenth-note passage ahead. To play the next passage, use a "cheat"* stroke! Utilizing a hard plastic mallet, play the next three measures on the suspended cymbal (positioned to your right) cutting off the sound as notated. Then for the next measure (the eighth note with the slash underneath), strike the left cymbal* which is cut off at the exact right moment by a colleague on your left, while you prepare yourself for the sixteenth-note passage to be played on the right suspended cymbal. Use a pre-set chair and dust pan directly under the right suspended cymbal. Place your foot upon the dust pan and use your knee to support, help control, and mute the underside of the suspended cymbal, while you play the passage with two hard plastic bell mallets. Again, as in Example 12, p. 14, play on the cymbal directly over the knee. Play aggressively into the cymbal in a *marcato* style. These particular measures may in fact be easier to play with the cymbal mounted on a normal suspended cymbal stand. Make sure to articulate and accentuate the rhythm by adding a bit of an accent on the next two downbeats. Then immediately return to the crash cymbals at four measures before letter **M**. This exact passage is repeated once more in the piece.

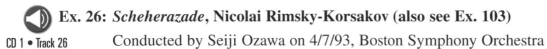

Ex. 26: *Scheherazade*, **Nicolai Rimsky-Korsakov (also see Ex. 103)**

CD 1 • Track 26   Conducted by Seiji Ozawa on 4/7/93, Boston Symphony Orchestra

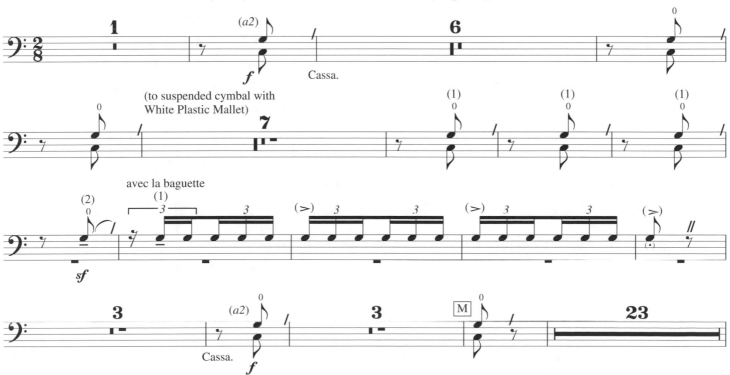

JEAN SIBELIUS

In *Finlandia*, by Sibelius (Example 27), the clear indications of rests and notes must be observed. Play all the rests and add a quick rest between the three measures of whole notes. This helps to create a clean attack for each of these measures. Two measures later, it may be appropriate to take a personal liberty: play all of the eighth notes exactly as written, including the rests, except for the last eighth note which is let to ring so that the energy of that note passes over the double bar and into the final section of the piece.

Ex. 27: *Finlandia*, **Jean Sibelius**

CD 1 • Track 27   Conducted by Ronald Feldman on 5/30/91, Boston Pops Orchestra

SERGEI RACHMANINOFF

The cymbal part in Rachmaninoff's Piano Concerto No. 2 (Ex. 28) is a well-known excerpt required for most percussion auditions. Perhaps the best way to play this is to use a larger rather than smaller pair of cymbals. The lower pitch of a 19" or 20" cymbal makes for a better blend with the ensemble sound source. In this excerpt there are no secrets. A clean and beautiful *pianissimo* stroke is all that is needed. Keep the piano's passing triplet figure clearly in mind when performing this piece. Your cymbals should be absolutely perpendicular to the floor, with a minimum amount of space between the two cymbals. Aim for a very specific place, add the smallest amount of slide possible, and as gently as possible make a brush-like stroke. Keeping the cymbals as close together as possible for the entire passage, and trying to play all the notes including the eighth notes as evenly as possible are the challenges. Though this passage is considered to be rhythmical, do not muffle any of the quarter notes. Instead, let all notes ring through, except for the very last note in the passage, the eighth note, which initiates the following "Allegro scherzando" section. Play this more like a short eighth note, and immediately cut it off.

Ex. 28: Piano Concerto No. 2, Mvt. 3, Sergei Rachmaninoff

CD 1 • Track 28   Conducted by Seiji Ozawa on 4/1/00, Boston Symphony Orchestra, Soloist: Nelson Freire

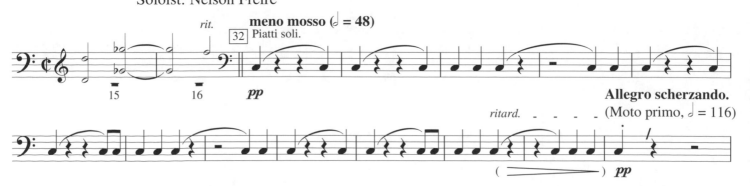

Suspended Cymbals

Before continuing the discussion of excerpts from the great composers, it is important to take a moment to look at suspended cymbals in more detail. Suspended cymbals hang horizontally and, because of their static position, accentuate calmness and tranquility. At the same time, suspended cymbals can highlight the mysteriousness of a piece. They can support short and long orchestral crescendos, add flashes of color, and when needed, create the most terrifying noise. They can also provide rhythmic underpinning when necessary.

GUSTAV MAHLER

A common favorite suspended cymbal part in the repertoire occurs in Mahler's First Symphony (Example 29), at the end of the third movement and leading into the fourth movement. The brilliantly conceived third movement opens with the famous tympani solo accompanying the "Frère Jacques" melody and concludes in a quiet, dirge-like way with cymbals and tam tam alternating strokes in a duet-like fashion. The nature of the melody (as well as the register of oboe and bassoon) creates the perfect opportunity for using two cymbals—one high, and the other a lower sounding cymbal—to better match the undulating texture. Using two suspended cymbals, even though only one is called for, try to accentuate the high and low quality of the music, as the music breathes in and out, finally dying out into a deep slumber. This may help to create a bit more interest in the line before concentrating on the softest strokes possible for the last seven measures of the movement. It also sets up the dozing listener for one of the great musical surprises in the entire literature. And the cymbal player does it all! Notice the *attacca* into Movement IV and the dynamic (*fff*)!! Finally, one must be careful to observe the composer's suggestion for mallet choice: Schwammschlägel, wound mallet; and Holzschlägel, wood (snare) stick.

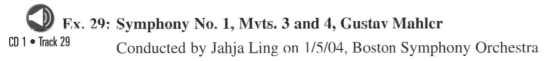

Ex. 29: Symphony No. 1, Mvts. 3 and 4, Gustav Mahler

CD 1 • Track 29   Conducted by Jahja Ling on 1/5/04, Boston Symphony Orchestra

IGOR STRAVINSKY

Igor Stravinsky's *Firebird Suite* (Example 30), at number **174**, offers another opportunity to utilize two suspended cymbals in order to enhance and support the melodic line. Here the musical gesture is repeated twice, once high and the second time at a lower pitch. Again, the gesture is like one taking a giant breath in and out. Using two different suspended cymbals (high and low) adds another dimension to the music.

Ex. 30: *Firebird*, **Igor Stravinsky**

CD 1 • Track 30
Conducted by Charles Dutoit on 4/27/98, Boston Symphony Orchestra

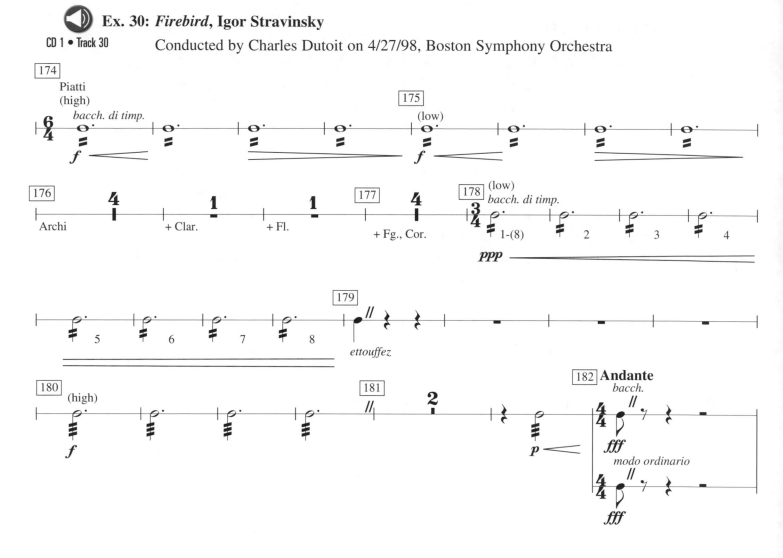

MAURICE RAVEL

Ravel's *Alborada del Grazioso* (Example 31) is an orchestral jewel of the crown if ever there was one. One of the most perfectly constructed works for orchestra, the music evokes both the mystery and beauty of Spanish life. The dance-like sections of the two outer movements are full of crisp and articulated percussion writing. All the parts are both challenging and fulfilling. This cymbal part calls for crisp, rhythmic finger-like snaps as well as soft splashes of color in the more elegant and subdued sections. The short cymbal snaps accompany the castanets at four measures after rehearsal number **3**. Note the word "slit" in the fourth and fifth measures. For an explanation of the "Slit Stroke," refer to Chapter Five, Cymbalism number 17. Large cymbal clashes occur during the passionate outbursts at number **16** (Ex. 32).

Ex. 31: *Alborada del Gracioso*, **Maurice Ravel**

CD 1 • Track 31 — Conducted by Bernard Haitink on 4/20/96, Boston Symphony Orchestra

 Ex. 32: *Alborada del Gracioso*, **Maurice Ravel**

CD 1 • Track 32 — Conducted by Bernard Haitink on 4/20/96, Boston Symphony Orchestra

In Example 33, after much soul-searching and score-searching, it was decided that the half notes should ring over the bar line until the third count of the next measure, and end together with the last quarter note of the snare drum line, thus helping to make the two-bar phrase more clear. However, at the end of the phrase at three measures before **10**, the half note should be played as a quarter note and cut off.

 Ex. 33: *Alborada del Gracioso*, **Maurice Ravel**

CD 1 • Track 33 — Conducted by Bernard Haitink on 4/20/96, Boston Symphony Orchestra

Looking ahead to Example 34, at rehearsal number **14**, use the tip of a light snare drum stick on a dark cymbal to evoke the mysterious and nervous, quivering quality of the passage.

Ex. 34: *Alborada del Gracioso*, **Maurice Ravel**

CD 1 • Track 34 Conducted by Bernard Haitink on 4/20/96, Boston Symphony Orchestra

In Example 35, at rehearsal number **28** the four eighth notes in the cymbal part should ring until the bar line. The only explanation for this is that it sounds correct.

Ex. 35: *Alborada del Gracioso*, **Maurice Ravel**

CD 1 • Track 35 Conducted by Bernard Haitink on 4/20/96, Boston Symphony Orchestra

Finally, in Example 36, it is at the end of the music at rehearsal number **34** where the orchestra explodes and the cymbal part simply goes wild! Play this entirely on smaller crash cymbals having a higher pitch (17" or 18"), and roll through the tremolo passages with two cymbals, making as much noise as you can. Then, in preparation for the last measure, quickly pick up a larger set and give it a good wallop. This piece is fun to play!

Ex. 36: *Alborada del Gracioso*, Maurice Ravel

Conducted by Bernard Haitink on 4/20/96, Boston Symphony Orchestra

FRANZ VON SUPPÉ AND JOHN PHILIP SOUSA

There are so many fine overtures by Gioacchino Rossini and Franz von Suppé. Although the cymbal parts are important components of these pieces, sometimes they are not listed in the score. The tradition is to simply double the bass drum part. A favorite of these overtures is one by Franz von Suppé entitled "Light Cavalry Overture" (Example 37). In the excerpt you see the bass drum part that the cymbal player is expected to simply double. Typically one would expect to play a note at the beginning and end of the rolls in measures 5 and 11, a *ff* at the beginning of the roll, and a short *mf* crash on the tied downbeat of the next measure.

Ex. 37: *Light Cavalry Overture,* **Franz von Suppé**

CD 1 • Track 37   Conducted by John Williams on 5/19/90, Boston Pops Orchestra

The interesting part, however, is at the 6/8 "Allegretto brilliante" section in Example 38. The music is light-hearted in nature. The repeated quarter notes take on a whole new character if one uses alternating down- and up-strokes. Repeated down-strokes could sound heavy and tense, but a more relaxed, swinging, and jocular bouncing type of playing is preferred. Play the down- and up-stroke pattern throughout the passage, thus causing an accented note on an occasional down-stroke and on one important up-stroke in the eighth measure.

 Ex. 38: *Light Cavalry Overture,* **Franz von Suppé**

CD 1 • Track 38   Conducted by John Williams on 5/19/90, Boston Pops Orchestra

At letter **C**, however, briefly inject three emphatic down-strokes, and then go back for two measures of down- and up-strokes. Repeat this pattern for the next four measures. Beginning with the dotted half note in the tenth measure of **C** up to letter **D**, continue to play only down-strokes. Much has been said about cymbal players using either the down-stroke or the up-stroke. Here in this overture there is a wonderful opportunity to use both! Except as shown, let all notes ring. The accents in parentheses are an addition, and help bring out a more musical performance. The letters above the notes indicate down-strokes and up-strokes. The use of small letters and capital letters are employed to simultaneously show the relative dynamic of the intended note (i.e., large notes are loud and small notes are softer).

The same interpretation markings apply as well to "The Stars and Stripes Forever" by John Philip Sousa (Example 39). This must be the most often performed march in the history of music. And what a great march it is! In order to capture the swing of this march, again use a combination of down- and up-strokes.

Ex. 39: "The Stars and Stripes Forever," John Philip Sousa

CD 1 • Track 39   Conducted by John Williams on 5/19/90, Boston Pops Orchestra

Chapter Five

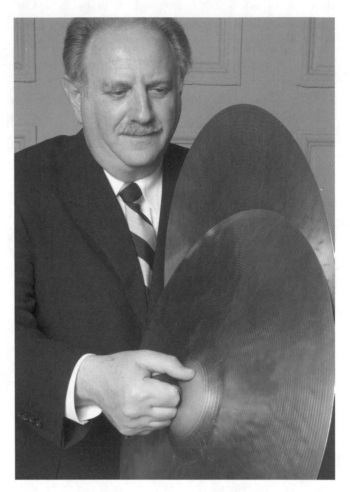

TWENTY-TWO CYMBALISMS

SPECIAL EFFECT STROKES FOR THE ORCHESTRAL CYMBAL PLAYER

In order to satisfy the demands of a wide variety of musical situations, the symphonic cymbalist will be aided by an array of special-effect strokes that have been categorized as "Cymbalisms." There are at least twenty-two special strokes, primarily used to create special soft sounds involving a variety of slide effects on different parts of the cymbal, as well as a number of special strokes for louder sounds. In order to remember them, each stroke has been given a name, onomatopoeic in nature, meaning that the name of the stroke is somewhat related to the sound produced.

However, it is the softer strokes that require the utmost in musical sensitivity and which are, because of their subtle differences and application, often the most interesting. One needs excellent cymbals for these special-effect strokes. All of the specialized slide strokes rely on taking advantage of the ridges or grooves on the inside of the cymbal, left intact after they are lathed as part of the normal cymbal-making process. In general, the new buffed or polished cymbals will *not* work for some of these specialized techniques.

Generally speaking, the strokes are created by manipulating two cymbals and can be grouped in two divisions: those that are produced by an ascending motion, and those that are produced by a descending motion. The ascending or upward strokes usually begin softly and end more loudly. The descending or downward strokes begin loudly and make a natural decrescendo. This is an important consideration when determining which stroke to use. More important is the nature of the musical gesture one is trying to create: is it to be exclamatory, declamatory, active or passive, gentle or aggressive?

1. The Zischend

Perhaps the most common slide stroke was coined by Richard Strauss in his virtuosic orchestral tone poem, *Ein Heldenleben*. Here Strauss calls for a **Zischend** stroke meaning, in this case, to slide or gently scrape the edge of one cymbal against the inner surface of the other in an upward brushing motion (In Example 40, the word *"Zischend"* in parentheses is an engraved part of the score).

 Ex. 40: *Ein Heldenleben*, **Richard Strauss**

Conducted by Seiji Ozawa on 2/10/95, Boston Symphony Orchestra

Ordinarily this is an easy stroke to accomplish, except that the speed and timing of the slide must precisely fit the musical gesture of the moment. In this case the nature of the gesture is one of speed. The entire slide should be accomplished within the space of one sixteenth note, so as to dovetail with the preceding sixteenth notes played by the flute, three measures before **14** in Example 40 and again, with the speed of the passing triplet after **20** in Example 41.

 Ex. 41: *Ein Heldenleben*, **Richard Strauss**

CD 2 • Track 2 Conducted by Seiji Ozawa on 2/10/95, Boston Symphony Orchestra

The "Cecil B. de Mille" slide stroke of all time can be found in the Berlioz *Requiem*. Hector Berlioz, the famous French Romantic composer, asks for huge forces of singers, instrumentalists, and auxilliary brass bands stationed about the concert hall. The score also calls for thirteen tympani players and as many cymbal players. With the availability of

Chapter Five: Twenty-two Cymbalisms   **47**

modern tympani, which can be re-tuned quickly and effectively, just six tympanists can adequately cover the part. Each tympanist is then asked to play the cymbals as well. Typically, the tympanists are lined up behind the orchestra in a long line stretching clear across the stage. Each player has a suspended cymbal and a pair of crash cymbals.

Ex. 42: *Requiem*, Hector Berlioz

CD 2 • Track 3 Conducted by Seiji Ozawa on 8/5/95, Soloist: Vincent Cole

There are only two notes on suspended cymbal in the piece, and they are very loud. However, in the most solemn music of the entire piece (the "Sanctus"), the six pairs of crash cymbals are stroked at the same time, and as softly as possible to accompany a chorus and tenor solo. Though the part suggests playing the cymbals in the normal way, using a *Zischend* stroke instead simplifies playing a unison *pianissimo*. The effect of this ultimate unison slide stroke, or *Zischend* stroke, is so extraordinary that reviewers often

mention it. Anthony Thomasini of *The Boston Globe*, in his review of the Boston Symphony's performance of October 21, 1993, wrote: "The cymbals are gently brushed together as the sopranos sustain hushed tones, and for a moment you wonder if that was an instrumental effect or were the sopranos whispering?"

2. The Hiss

In Gustav Mahler's Symphony No. 2, "The Resurrection," one of the most profound and moving symphonies of the late Nineteenth Century, there exists one of the finest moments of the entire cymbal repertoire. It is one single, *pianissimo* stroke.

Ex. 43: Symphony No. 2, Mvt. 5, Gustav Mahler

CD 2 • Track 4 — Conducted by Seiji Ozawa on 10/2/99, Boston Symphony Orchestra

A hushed entrance of the chorale theme presented by the brass is followed by a measure of pizzicato in the strings, and then this exquisite, *pianissimo* cymbal stroke. For

this magical moment one may employ a stroke called the **Hiss**. This is done initially, by carefully and quietly pre-setting the extreme edge of the right cymbal against the extreme edge of the left cymbal. Then, at the precise moment, slide the edge of the right cymbal in an upward motion along the edge of the left cymbal, and then separate the two cymbals from one another at the end of the slide. It is a very soft slide with a bit of edge or "hiss." The orchestra must be very quiet, and the hall should have good acoustics for this stroke to be successful.

Among the most beautiful endings of any piece is the moment at the end of *Fêtes* (Example 44) by Debussy. A low and grumbling bass passage followed by three clear bell-like tympani tones, and a moment of silence precedes a perfect setting for a *Hiss* stroke. Though somewhat less dramatic, the sheer beauty of this moment is not unlike the moment in Mahler's Symphony No. 2 (see Example 43). This wisp of sound into the air when properly executed will always cause appreciative heads to turn.

Ex. 44: *Fêtes, from Nocturnes*, Claude Debussy
CD 2 • Track 5 — Conducted by Charles Dutoit on 8/9/92, Boston Symphony Orchestra

3. The Swish

The **Swish** stroke is similar to the *Hiss* stroke. However, it is a bit louder and therefore perhaps more useful. The *Swish* stroke is accomplished by placing the top edge of the right cymbal near the bottom inside edge (about one inch from the outer edge) of the left cymbal and gently scraping from bottom to top on the left cymbal, following the circumference of the edge of the cymbal. Because one has the entire circumference of the cymbal available for scraping, a long scrape, either slow or fast, is possible. The sound is louder than the *Hiss* stroke, softer than a regular *Zischend* stroke, yet longer in duration, while it produces a fast, agile, and flowing gesture. There are a number of places to use this stroke. In fact, any traditional *Zischend* stroke, where the abrupt short span of the *Zischend* stroke is less than desirable, could be substituted by a *Swish* stroke.

In a recent performance of *Ein Heldenleben* (Example 41), the conductor, Bernard Haitink, asked for a longer and more sinister sound than a normal *Zischend* stroke would otherwise provide. By using the *Swish* stroke, a most satisfying thumbs-up sign was flashed back at me!

Another perfect spot for the *Swish* stroke is in Richard Wagner's *Götterdämmerung, Act Three.*

Ex. 45: *Götterdämmerung, Act 3*, **Richard Wagner**

CD 2 • Track 6

Conducted by Bernard Haitink on 4/30/94, Boston Symphony Orchestra, Soloist: Jane Eaglend

4. The Swirl

Though infrequently used, the **Swirl** stroke is one of this author's favorites. One can start this stroke just about anywhere on the cymbal. It is a slide that can begin with a normal stroke, or like a *Swish*, or a *Whizz* stroke (see Cymbalisms 3 and 9). The stroke continues on around and about the circumference of the left cymbal, first moving down,

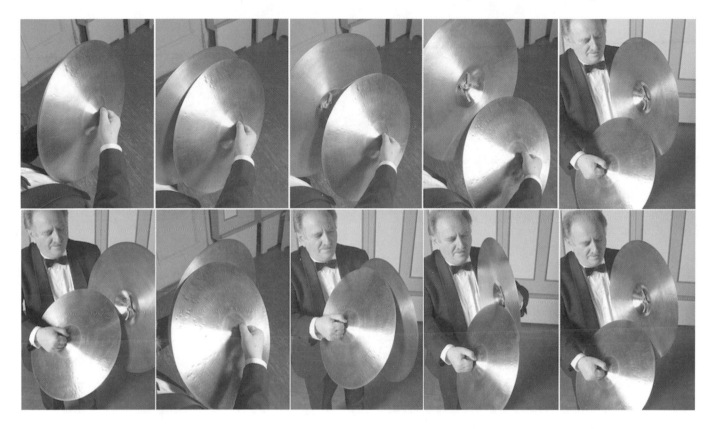

then up, and down again. It can continue indefinitely, and then finish by lifting off the cymbal. It can stop suddenly on the cymbal, or it can finish by first slowing down and then stopping on the cymbal. The left (or stationary) cymbal must shift angles as the right (moving cymbal) moves against it. The left cymbal must lean toward the right as the right cymbal moves up, and then it must lean to the left as the right cymbal moves down, thus allowing for sufficient friction during the process.

The *Swirl* stroke can be used for any note with a hold over it. One example for this stroke is the Boston Pops tune "Good Swing Wenceslas" (Example 46), arranged by Sammy Nestico. It can also be used successfully on the last note of Britten's Violin Concerto No. 1 (see Example 58).

Ex. 46: "Good Swing Wenceslas," arranged by Sammy Nestico

CD 2 • Track 7   Conducted by Keith Lockhart on 12/15/98, Boston Pops Orchestra

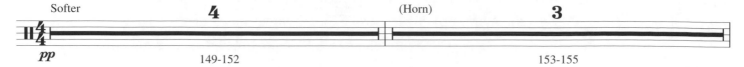

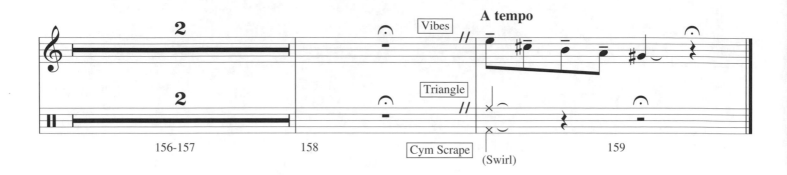

5. The Frizzle

Dvořák's Symphony No. 9 offers an opportunity for either a *Frizzle* stroke, a *Zischend* stroke, or a *Swirl* stroke. Dvořák's music—otherwise rhythmic, vital, and intense—here shifts to a gentler and quieter mood, subsiding into a gently, rocking motion, setting up the moment for one of the most amazing cymbal strokes in the entire repertoire. In the **Frizzle** stroke, the cymbals are stroked together very softly, in a normal manner, after which the player slides or scrapes the top edge of one cymbal against the inside of the other in a downward motion. The sound is fuller, has more body, and is more pronounced than a *Zischend*. Once a *Frizzle* stroke is executed, one could proceed directly into a *Swirl* stroke, thereby extending the slide stroke for the entire notated duration. The *Frizzle* and *Swirl* stroke combination has been used successfully many times. The effect in Dvořák's Symphony No. 9 is at once dramatic and subdued, a truly magical moment!

Ex. 47: Symphony No. 9, Mvt. 4, Antonín Dvořák

CD 2 • Track 8   Conducted by James Levine on 9/30/06, Boston Symphony Orchestra

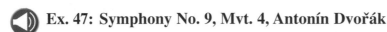

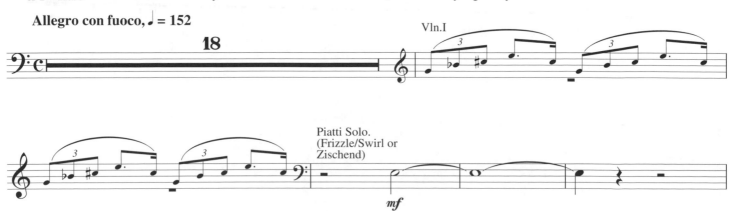

Another such rare moment featuring a percussion instrument in a similar, yet unique way would be the *tam tam* stroke in the fourth movement of Tschaikowsky's Symphony No. 6 (not a *Frizzle* stroke example).

Ex. 48: Symphony No. 6, Mvt. 4 (mm. 134–139), Peter I. Tschaikowsky

CD 2 • Track 9

Conducted by Seiji Ozawa on 4/26/86, Boston Symphony Orchestra

The only other comparable musical moment of *similar intensity* is the famous tympani stroke ten measures before the ending of the Funeral March movement of Beethoven's "Eroica Symphony" (not a *Frizzle* stroke example).

Ex. 49: Symphony No. 3, "Eroica," Mvt. 2 (mm. 236–241), Ludwig van Beethoven

CD 2 • Track 10 Conducted by James Levine on 11/20/04, Boston Symphony Orchestra

Another example of the use of the *Frizzle* stroke is in Richard Strauss's epic musical setting of *Don Quixote*. In the fifth bar of rehearsal number **27**, there is a *piano* note where a *Frizzle* stroke can be used. The orchestration is a bit thicker here than before, and this allows the player to "stretch" the cymbal sound over the full quarter note, thus more fully supporting the cello solo.

Ex. 50: *Don Quixote*, **Richard Strauss**

CD 2 • Track 11 Conducted by Seiji Ozawa on 2/23/01, Boston Symphony Orchestra, Soloists: Yo Yo Ma/Steve Ansell

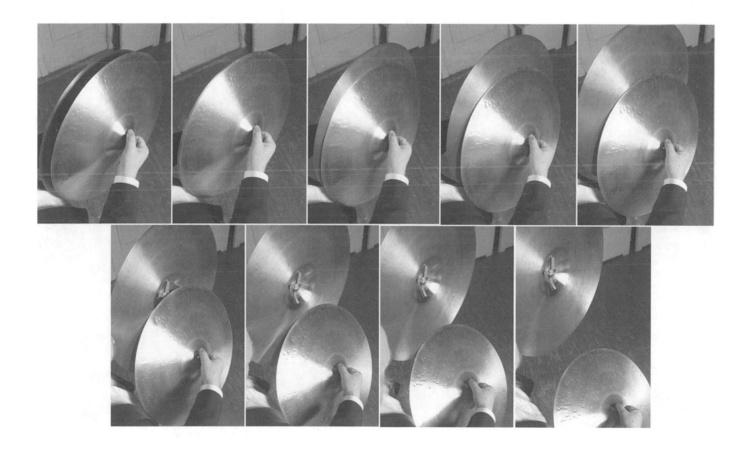

6. The Frizz

In Igor Stravinsky's *Petrouchka* one can employ a stroke called a **Frizz**. This stroke is produced exactly the same as the *Frizzle* was in the example from Dvořák's Symphony No. 9, except that the stroke is stopped midway while both cymbals are still in contact. Moving both cymbals simultaneously into the chest during the most active part of the slide creates an unusual silence. The effect is like tearing a piece of paper in half, but stopping in the middle of the tear. The attention drawn by the stopping of the activity is what creates the interest.

Ex. 51: *Petrouchka (1947 version)*, **Igor Stravinsky**

CD 2 • Track 12   Conducted by Charles Dutoit on 8/24/04, Boston Symphony Orchestra

7. The Grizzle

Claude Debussy, in his famous work, *La Mer*, offers the orchestral cymbalist some of the most interesting opportunities incorporating the sound of suspended cymbals to simulate the sound of splashing water and roaring waves.

However, in order to capture or emulate the sound of stopped French horns at two measures before rehearsal number **48**, yet another variation is incorporated on the slide stroke. This one is called a **Grizzle**. It is produced by bringing two cymbals together softly as in a normal *pianissimo* stroke, then sliding the whole surface of one cymbal down the whole of the other in a downward motion. The sound is thicker and rougher than the *Frizzle* stroke.

Note well that in this particular excerpt it is *necessary* to carry two suspended cymbal mallets in the right hand while performing the *Grizzle* stroke during the first six measures of number **48**. During the sixth measure the cymbals should be quickly dropped on a table in preparation for the suspended roll in the next measure, two measures before **49**. Since there really is no time to properly drop the cymbals, the following action is suggested: let both cymbals "drop" vertically onto the table immediately after the *Grizzle* stroke is complete. Then let the right cymbal loose while it is balanced by the left, still in vertical position, and proceed to roll on the suspended cymbal, making a one-handed roll.

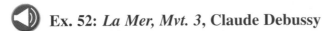

Ex. 52: *La Mer, Mvt. 3*, **Claude Debussy**

CD 2 • Track 13

Conducted by Robert Spano on 1/8/00, Boston Symphony Orchestra

8. The Grizz

The **Grizz** stroke is simply a short *Grizzle* stroke akin to the *Frizzle* and *Frizz* strokes. The *Grizz*, like the *Frizz* stroke, begins with a normal stroke. However, instead of pulling the cymbals apart, they remain in contact: the whole of one cymbal should slide down the whole of the other cymbal (in the *Frizz* stroke only the top edge of the cymbal maintains contact), then somewhere along the way it is abruptly stopped (while both cymbals are still in contact) by rolling both cymbals into the chest. The *Grizz* can be used in place of the *Frizz* when a slightly rougher or darker sound is desired. One may find the *Grizz* stroke to be useful in Bartók's *The Miraculous Mandarin*. See Example 61, where the *Grizz* stroke is used in combination with a *Prezz 2* stroke (Cymbalism 11).

9. The Whizz

Some of the best cymbal parts may be found in the music of English composers Edward Elgar and Ralph Vaughan Williams. The courtly style, the noble gesture, and the uplifting marches found in their symphonies and massive choral works often feature cymbals, bass drum, and snare drum, as well as tympani. These composers write with great boldness and utilize extreme dynamics ranging from *ffff* to *pppp*. In Vaughan Williams's *Sea Symphony*, a work for large chorus and symphony orchestra, these extreme dynamics are evident throughout the score.

Ex. 53: *A Sea Symphony, Mvt. 4*, **Ralph Vaughan Williams**

CD 2 • Track 14 — Conducted by Roger Norrington on 3/25/94, Boston Symphony Orchestra, Soloists: Janice Watson, Kevin McMillan, Tanglewood Festival Chorus

Example 53 shows part of the concluding section of this symphony. The soaring theme of the earlier movement is played in a brooding *adagio* as the symphony comes to a Mahlerian halt, but not before some extremely delicate and soft cymbal strokes are played. In order to capture the dying-away effect of the passage, a stroke was created called the **Whizz**. In this stroke, the two cymbals are carefully placed together. After an initial and quick slide gesture, and at the proper moment, one cymbal gently slides straight down and simultaneously out into the air. The effect is that of a gentle sigh.

Another possibility to use a *Whizz* stroke exists in Maurice Ravel's *Valses Nobles et Sentimentales*. The *Whizz* stroke here is quick, light, and graceful. Since the stroke is repeated a number of times, let the cymbals ring through the measure, cut if off at the bar line, and reset for another *Whizz* stroke. This stroke sounds just fine for the first line. After rehearsal number **32** and the repeat, the *Whizz* may become somewhat redundant and lose some of its magical aural and visual effects. However, the musical material is a direct repetition, and therefore so is the cymbal stroke.

Ex. 54: *Valses Nobles et Sentimentales*, **Maurice Ravel**

CD 2 • Track 15   Conducted by Seiji Ozawa on 12/6/97, Boston Symphony Orchestra

IV

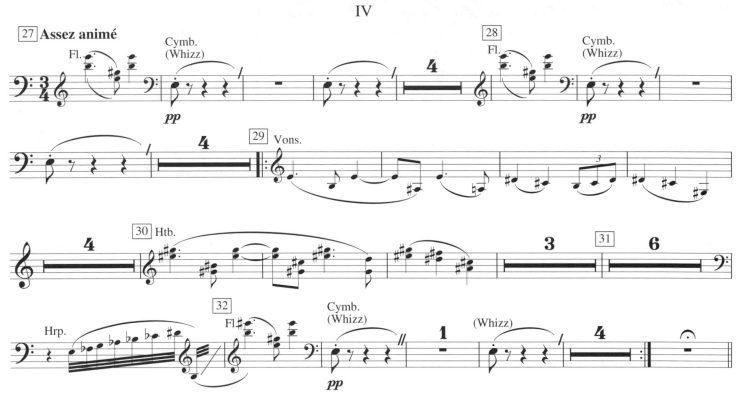

Richard Strauss's wonderful tone poem, *Don Quixote*, offers some of the finest possibilities for the cymbal player. A virtual treasure house of Cymbalisms is possible. First of all, consider the *bravura* closing section of the opening movement, which with an exciting salvo of cymbal color, sets our hero Don Quixote off to battle (Example 55).

Ex. 55: *Don Quixote*, **Richard Strauss**

CD 2 • Track 16   Conducted by Seiji Ozawa on 2/24/01, Boston Symphony Orchestra,
Soloists: Yo Yo Ma/Steve Ansell

"Variation I" features the return of a more reflective hero punctuated by a series of three *pianissimo* notes for which a *Whizz* stroke may be used. The *pianissimo* strokes throughout the piece are often difficult to place and control. Carefully selecting a combination of slide strokes facilitates much of the problem. At **20**, note the reference to a *Slice* stroke. This is described and explained in Cymbalism 16.

 Ex. 56: *Don Quixote*, Richard Strauss

CD 2 • Track 17   Conducted by Seiji Ozawa on 2/24/01, Boston Symphony Orchestra, Soloists: Yo Yo Ma/Steve Ansell

Var. 1. Gemächlich

Our hero dies at the end of the piece, and the last two measures poignantly and with full acceptance of his death, dramatize his final breath (in and out). Here a *Whizz* stroke may be utilized for the penultimate note, and a traditional *Zischend* stroke for the final note.

 Ex. 57: *Don Quixote*, Richard Strauss

CD 2 • Track 18   Conducted by Seiji Ozawa on 2/24/01, Boston Symphony Orchestra, Soloists: Yo Yo Ma/Steve Ansell

In Example 58, Britten's Concerto No. 1 for Violin and Orchestra, the *Whizz* stroke is employed in addition to natural strokes, and a final *Whizz/Swirl combination* stroke. Starting at three measures after **47**, following two measures of tympani Ds, there is a perfect opportunity to use the *Whizz* stroke, and then again, two measures later. For the next four entrances, play in a normal fashion, allowing for the required *crescendo*. In the subsequent two measures use the *Whizz* stroke followed by one normal stroke. For the final note use a combination *Whizz* and *Swirl* stroke. To accomplish this combination stroke begin with the cymbals together, but instead of moving the cymbals out into the air as in a typical *Whizz* stroke, keep them together and swirl first downward then upward. The right cymbal should move around the circumference of the left cymbal as you make a long, sustained diminuendo, while at the same time slowing down the motion of the *Swirl* until the sound simply ceases. The cymbals should remain in contact throughout the stroke and perfectly satisfy the musical gesture.

Ex. 58: Concerto No. 1 for Violin and Orchestra, Mvt. 3, Benjamin Britten

CD 2 • Track 19

Conducted by Paavo Berglund on 3/27/04, Boston Symphony Orchestra,
Soloist: Frank Peter Zimmermann

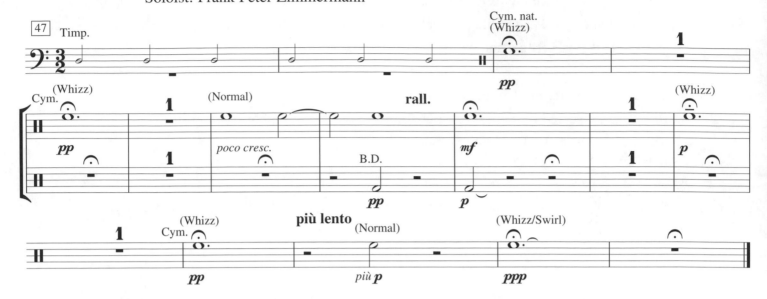

A similarly exposed cymbal part is found in Benjamin Britten's *War Requiem* (Example 59). The *War Requiem* is one of the most moving works of the twentieth century, and Britten employs an abundance of percussion sounds. Starting at rehearsal number **89** and continuing through number **92**, the crash cymbals are again used in the softest dynamics, this time accompanying a solo soprano along with a hushed choir. It is a long and difficult passage to play. The extended passage calls for repeated soft strokes, at a tempo slow enough that each note sounds as if it were the opening note in a piece. One must place the notes *precisely* in rhythm, maintain dynamic control (note the *crescendo* and *decrescendo*), and at the end of the passage make a *diminuendo* into a silent measure. The composer's instruction to use a *natural* or normal stroke is taken literally. The production of a beautiful *pianissimo* stroke is essential. The best results may be achieved by carefully stroking one cymbal just below the top edge of the other, and beginning the stroke at this specific spot every time.

Ex. 59: *War Requiem*, **Benjamin Britten**

CD 2 • Track 20

Conducted by Seiji Ozawa on 2/26/00, Boston Symphony Orchestra,
Soloists: Christine Goerke/TFC

10. The Prezz 1

Only recently performed by the Boston Symphony Orchestra, Dvořák's *Otello Overture* is a work this author had never played before. The piece is filled with some very difficult *pianissimo and pianississimo* strokes that come in quick succession. The conductor was very demanding and insisted on the most extreme *pianissimo* dynamic for every entrance. Having developed an array of strokes to help me out with other difficult choices, for this situation, I found the opportunity to create yet another kind of slide stroke.

Here we see three measures tied together, not unlike the solo cymbal measure in Dvořák's Symphony No. 9. There is virtually no convincing way to play these three measures on cymbals. The **Prezz 1** stroke discussed here resulted from a great deal of experimenting. Like the *Whizz* stroke, the *Prezz 1* stroke starts with the cymbals together. They are then pulled apart slowly, scraping the whole of one cymbal against the whole of the other (like the *Grizzle* stroke) over the entire length of the three measures.

Then there are only two quick measures of rest (at one beat per measure), to prepare for a *Hiss* stroke. Since the music is extremely delicate, all of this must be done quickly, quietly and efficiently.

Ex. 60: *Otello Overture*, **Antonín Dvořák**

CD 2 • Track 21
Conducted by Hans Graf on 7/23/04, Boston Symphony Orchestra

11. The Prezz 2

The Miraculous Mandarin (Example 61) offers additional challenging possibilities. Perhaps the most interesting effect occurs in the latter part of the orchestral suite. At rehearsal number **101**, Bartók's already gruesome music becomes lugubrious and lascivious.

In this ominous, dirge-like section, one might imagine some hideous monster advancing toward its innocent victim, ever so slowly, while dragging its club foot along the floor. The stroke that works best for this moment is a modified up-and-down *Prezz 1* stroke called a **Prezz 2** stroke. Begin the stroke with both cymbals together, slide one cymbal down slowly about three or four inches and stop on the cymbal as the left cymbal moves into the chest and the right cymbal into the stomach. Since the gesture is repeated immediately and continuously throughout the next seventeen measures, there is no time to recover. To play the next bar in time, simply move the cymbals away from the chest and slide the cymbals back up to the original starting position and again move both cymbals into the chest. This stroke is thus repeated for a total of eighteen measures. However, as the music gets louder, the stroke advances into a full *Grizz* stroke in measures five and six after number **102**, and then shifts immediately back into the *Prezz 2* stroke for the last three measures of the passage.

 Ex. 61: *The Miraculous Mandarin*, **Béla Bartók**

CD 2 • Track 22   Conducted by Seiji Ozawa on 2/4/94, Boston Symphony Orchestra

12. The Roll

Of the many cymbal effects that are possible, none is more unusual than the *a duè* cymbal roll. The **Roll** is accomplished by moving one cymbal around the circumference of the other while keeping the cymbals in constant contact, and without crossing over the center of either cymbal (otherwise an air pocket may result). In the fourth movement of Zoltán Kodály's *Háry János Suite*, entitled "Battle and Defeat of Napoleon" (Example 62), the cymbals are first struck and then joined together for a *Roll*.)

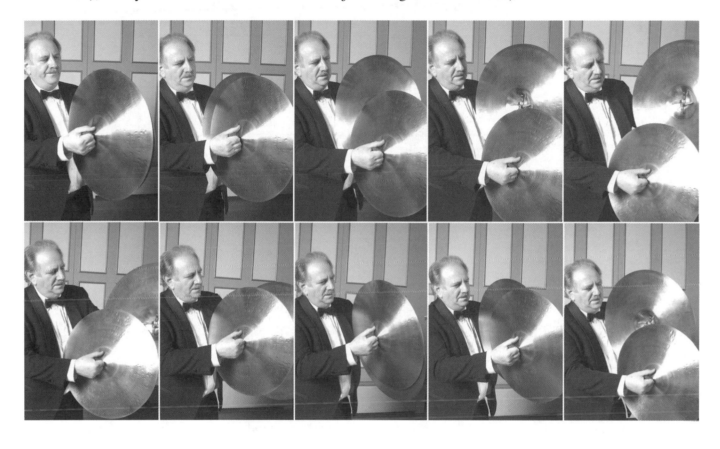

Ex. 62: *Háry János Suite, Mvt. 4*, **Zoltán Kodály**

CD 2 • Track 23   Conducted by Kurt Masur on 8/10/85, Boston Symphony Orchestra

Perhaps an equally unique moment occurs in Béla Bartók's *The Miraculous Mandarin*. Here the cymbalist is asked to roll on a pair of cymbals (*Piatti a 2*) for a total of sixteen measures while making a deafening crescendo! This crescendo becomes so loud that back-up reinforcement is necessary. Therefore, after approximately three measures of rolling with two cymbals, another player "sneaks in" with a set of hi-hat cymbals. The hi-hats are loosely set so that a continuous sizzle sound is heard when rolled with two suspended cymbal mallets. This hi-hat sound can get extremely loud, so care must be taken not to cover over the vigorous activity of the main cymbal player until the last two measures of the crescendo.

Ex. 63: *The Miraculous Mandarin,* **Béla Bartók**

CD 2 • Track 24   Conducted by Seiji Ozawa on 2/4/94, Boston Symphony Orchestra

13. The Crusher

The Miraculous Mandarin (Example 64) of Béla Bartók continues to offer yet another interesting Cymbalistic possibility. The fourth through the eighth measures of number **36** indicate Bartók's note to use two cymbals and make a *tremolo*.

Since there is relatively little time for making an *a2* cymbal roll (only two and a half beats in total), use this next stroke called the **Crusher**. An effective way to accomplish this stroke is by bringing two 20" cymbals together with tremendous force while creating a considerable flam (made top to bottom). Keep the cymbals together for the length of the measure while moving them around and about in a circular fashion, letting them sizzle. The sound—repeated five times in a row—is harsh, if not ugly, and precisely what the composer must have had in mind. It is suggested that the quarter-note stroke preceding the crash strokes seven measures before **C** should be played with a snare drum stick by another player. The struck cymbal followed immediately by the *Crusher* stroke accentuates this section beautifully.

Ex. 64: *The Miraculous Mandarin*, **Béla Bartók**

Conducted by Seiji Ozawa on 10/31/98, Boston Symphony Orchestra

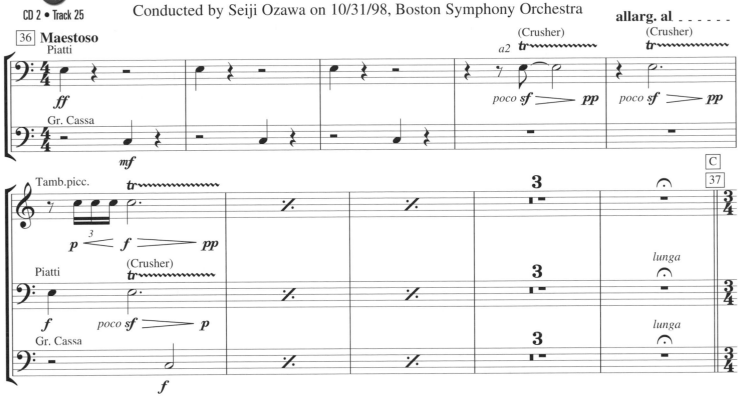

14. The Sizzle

In the *Scottish Fantasy* of Max Bruch (Example 65), the difficulty lies in the extended and repeated use of cymbals in a *pianissimo* dynamic at a slow tempo. To accomplish this task, a very short **Sizzle** stroke may be used. Crush the attack just a bit with little or no slide, one quarter of an inch at most. Instead of releasing all horizontal pressure once contact is made, maintain just enough pressure to keep the cymbals in contact, thereby allowing them to continue vibrating against each other. The effect of this stroke is that it obscures the contact sound completely while it helps to darken the overall sound. Playing these extremely soft dynamics, at a very slow tempo, in the context of a very slow beat pattern, can be nerve-wracking. Another interpretation of these same musical notes uses another Cymbalism: the *Single Flap*. This stroke is discussed in detail in Cymbalism 18.

Ex. 65: *Scottish Fantasy*, **Max Bruch**

Conducted by Roger Norrington on 7/5/92, Boston Symphony Orchestra,
Soloist: Midori

A similar situation exists in the opening of Benjamin Britten's Concerto No. 1 for Violin and Orchestra. Examples 66 and 67 may well be the most difficult and most delicate in the entire cymbal literature. Here the number and level of problems are several and complex. This most unusual opening—utilizing only tympani and a pair of crash cymbals—sets the stage for one of the most beautifully crafted pieces in the repertoire. The opening is absolutely stunning in its originality and conception. Perhaps only Beethoven with the four-note tympani opening of his violin concerto achieves similar status. As you can see in Example 66, the concerto opens with a delicate tympani figure answered by a lone cymbal note. The *Sizzle* stroke may be effective here, in this gesture that is repeated three times, with no other instruments playing. Note the subtle *crescendo*.

Ex. 66: Concerto No. 1 for Violin and Orchestra, Mvt. 1, Benjamin Britten

CD 2 • Track 27 Conducted by Paavo Berglund on 3/27/04, Boston Symphony Orchestra, Soloist: Frank Peter Zimmermann

In Example 67, Britten presents the same thematic material: tympani answered by a cymbal note. The material is repeated for twelve measures, but this time it is accompanied by a gentle solo violin *obbligato*. Again, this is a good place to use the *Sizzle* stroke throughout.

Ex. 67: Concerto No. 1 for Violin and Orchestra, Mvt. 1, Benjamin Britten

CD 2 • Track 28 Conducted by Paavo Berglund on 3/27/04, Boston Symphony Orchestra, Soloist: Frank Peter Zimmermann

15. The Kiss

The **Kiss** stroke is not a slide stroke, but a rather direct, quick in-and-outward stroke. Start out by placing both cymbals in perfect alignment, about a half-inch apart (further apart for louder volumes and closer together for softer). Perform a quick in-and-out motion, making full contact for just an instant, then immediately pull away. The result is a quick, clean stroke without any slide grace note or flam sound.

Used sparingly for both soft and loud strokes, it is a very useful and interesting sound. Though there are a number of places to use this stroke, it is recommended you not use this stroke more than once in any given piece. A good place to use this stroke is in Richard Wagner's *Siegfried's Rhein Journey*.

Ex. 68: *Siegfried's Rhein Journey*, **Richard Wagner**

CD 2 • Track 29   Conducted by Seiji Ozawa on 9/29/99, Boston Symphony Orchestra

Two other excellent spots to use the stroke occur in Maurice Ravel's *La Valse*, and in Gustav Mahler's Symphony No. 9.

Ex. 69: *La Valse*, **Maurice Ravel**

CD 2 • Track 30   Conducted by Seiji Ozawa on 12/6/97, Boston Symphony Orchestra

Ex. 70: Symphony No. 9, Mvt. 3, Gustav Mahler

CD 2 • Track 31   Conducted by Bernard Haitink on 11/11/95, Boston Symphony Orchestra

16. The Slice Stroke

17. The Slit Stroke

In the opening of the fourth movement of Rimsky-Korsakov's *Scheherazade*, all notes are marked as quarter notes, but in fact, the first two notes should be played shorter than the printed values. The third note is precisely notated and should be cut off as indicated in Example 71. The fourth through the seventh notes are a bit longer than the printed note values. A **Slice** stroke may be used to play the first two notes. This stroke is generally used for loud, short notes. It is a normal stroke except that the preparation for the stroke is more vertical. The exact dynamics required will determine how far the two cymbals are apart before making contact. For a typical forte stroke, the cymbals are about three inches apart with the right cymbal above the left. After contact is made, the two cymbals come apart for just a second before they are vigorously pulled into the chest for a fast and quick stop.

Ex 71: *Scheherazade*, **Nicolai Rimsky-Korsakov**

CD 2 • Track 32   Conducted by Seiji Ozawa on 4/7/93, Boston Symphony Orchestra

Allegro molto e frenetico.

Later in the movement (Example 72), at letter **P**, one may employ a stroke called a **Slit**. The *Slit* stroke is extremely short and fast, and is generally used for loud and the most extreme short notes, though it is equally effective for soft notes. Preparation for the *Slit*

stroke is similar to that of the *Slide* stroke. However, after contact is made, they are not allowed to come apart. Immediately after contact is made, both cymbals are pulled into the chest. The *Slit* stroke, like the *Slice* stroke, can be used both for single notes or repeated notes. In

either case, it is made very aggressively. At letter **P** and again at letters **Q** through **R**, the cymbals are rolled into the chest immediately after contact is made. They are allowed to bounce off, to recover and re-position, to again make contact, to again quickly roll back into the chest, where they are once again aggressively stopped. In other words, two separate strokes are made to produce two separate eighth notes. At the ninth measure after **R**, one may use the *Slice* stroke once again for four measures, and then return to the *Slit* stroke for the next five measures. All the rests are strictly observed. The opening measures of Boston Pops favorite "Bugler's Holiday" also offer an excellent opportunity for the *Slit* stroke. See Example 80.

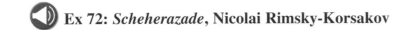

Ex 72: *Scheherazade*, **Nicolai Rimsky-Korsakov**

CD 2 • Track 33   Conducted by Seiji Ozawa on 4/7/93, Boston Symphony Orchestra

Another fine example of the *Slice* stroke occurs in Stravinsky's *Petrouchka* (1947). Here the two isolated notes in the cymbals part, one measure before **74** and one measure before **75**, are played with a full-bodied *Slice* stroke and create the perfect upbeat to the bass drum notes that follow on the downbeat of the next measure.

Ex. 73: *Petrouchka (1947 version)*, **Igor Stravinsky**

CD 2 • Track 34

Conducted by Charles Dutoit on 8/24/04, Boston Symphony Orchestra

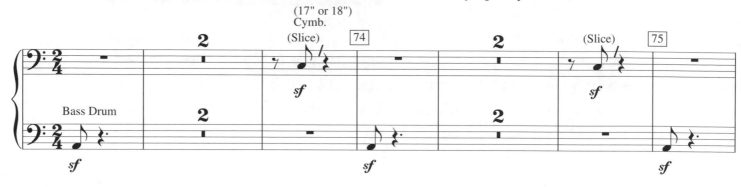

"Ballet of the Unhatched Chicks," from *Pictures at an Exhibition* by Moussorgsky/Ravel represents a unique example for the use of a *Slit* stroke in a soft passage. A very small pair of cymbals are recommended, no larger than 10" to 14". To accomplish this, allow the cymbal to make contact with each other immediately before bringing both cymbals into your chest. When successful, the otherwise risky attempt here is very satisfying. Trying to control the dynamic evenly for the four notes is the difficulty.

Ex. 74: *Pictures at an Exhibition, "V. Ballet of the Unhatched Chicks,"*

CD 2 • Track 35

Modeste Moussorgsky/Ravel

Conducted by Charles Dutoit on 8/22/98, Boston Symphony Orchestra

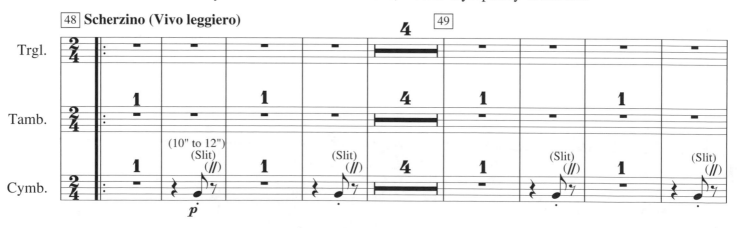

In Example 75, the same small cymbals are used, employing a normal stroke, thus helping to create a wonderful toy-like mix of triangle, tambourine, and cymbal sound. At **55a**, we have a return to the original interpretation of producing a soft and short ***pppp*** *Slit* stroke.

CD 2 • Track 36 **Ex. 75:** *Pictures at an Exhibition, "V. Ballet of the Unhatched Chicks,"*
Modeste Moussorgsky/Ravel
Conducted by Charles Dutoit on 8/22/98, Boston Symphony Orchestra

In Example 76, "The Market" (Movement VII), of the same piece by Moussorgsky/Ravel, there are more examples of the *Slice* stroke at three different dynamic levels: ***mp***, ***p***, and ***f***. Note the two measures before **69** where a quick roll (frottées) of the two cymbals is required, which is immediately followed by a *Slit* stroke. (For a fuller explanation of the *Roll*, see Cymbalism 12). Finally, at number **71**, one must quickly and quietly drop the crash cymbals on a table and pick up a mallet to play the following measure. All of this must be done during the *tutti* rest preceding measure **71**!— a delicate maneuver, to be sure.

Ex. 76: *Pictures at an Exhibition, "VII. Limoges – The Market,"*

CD 2 • Track 37   **Modeste Moussorgsky/Ravel**

Conducted by Charles Dutoit on 8/22/98, Boston Symphony Orchestra

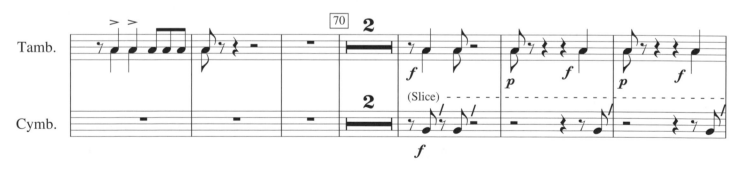

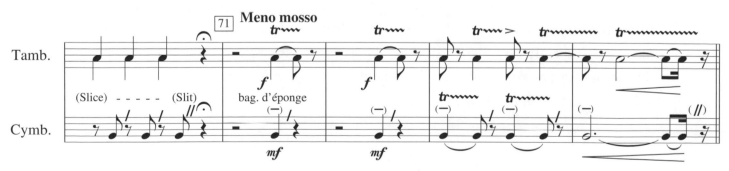

18. The Single Flap

The **Single Flap** stroke is a very useful stroke because it is so easily combined with other strokes. The *Single Flap* is initiated by placing both cymbals together, as in the *Whizz* and *Prezz I* strokes. At

the desired moment, the bottom of the right cymbal is lifted away from the left cymbal while maintaining contact at the top of the cymbals. The cymbals are then brought back together in preparation for a cleanly articulated, though slightly short, muffled and pointed attack.

The *Single Flap* stroke can be adapted to connect with a normal soft or loud crash. The *Frizzle*, the *Grizzle*, the *Prezz I*, the *Whizz*, or even the *Slice* and *Slit* strokes can be connected to the *Single Flap*. In each case the result is a slight "button" or accent on the attack. This is one versatile stroke. The *Single Flap* stroke can be used in Strauss's *Don Quixote* (Example 50), the Bruch *Scottish Fantasy* (Example 65), and others.

19. The Multi Flap

The **Multi Flap** stroke can be used with fast, reiterated strokes, but it is typically reserved for fast and loud strokes. It is essentially the same as the *Single Flap* stroke except that the technique takes some additional effort. Keeping the top of the two cymbals together, while the bottoms move out and back in to make contact, is referred to as a *Multi Flap* effect. The technique is aided by gripping the right-hand strap tightly, leaving a good half-inch between the grip and the cymbal.

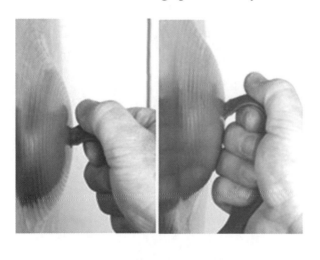

Then, as if knocking or rapping on a door, the cymbal is moved in and out in quick succession. This stroke must be timed precisely to be effective. It has been used in the conclusion of Tschaikowsky's Symphony No. 4 (Example 19), if and when the tempo becomes extremely fast. The *Multi Flap* stroke may be used successfully in the repeated eighth-note measures in Rossini's *Overture to William Tell* (Example 77).

At seven measures before **O**, a series of normal down-strokes is appropriate. At **O**, continue with two more measures of down-strokes, then follow that with two measures of *Multi Flap* strokes. This four-measure pattern is repeated, followed by four measures of *Slice* strokes, and then followed by a series of normal *sf* down-strokes, each of which is followed by a *Slit* stroke. However, this *Slit* stroke should be played here as an upstroke!

This gesture is repeated four times. Letter **P** repeats this entire process. All of the notes in this piece are in "tutti play," and so all must be played in strict unison with the brass. All rests must be strictly observed. Some exceptions may be made: measures 13, 15, and 17 after letter **O** and again after letter **P** may be allowed to ring through the entire measure. Take note that in each case, the long notes are followed by *Slit* strokes played as upstrokes. If you listen carefully to the music you will see why this makes good musical sense. Note that D and U mean down- or up-strokes.

Ex. 77: *Overture to "William Tell"*, **Gioacchini Rossini**

CD 2 • Track 38   Conducted by Miguel Harth-Bedoya on 7/27/03, Boston Pops Orchestra

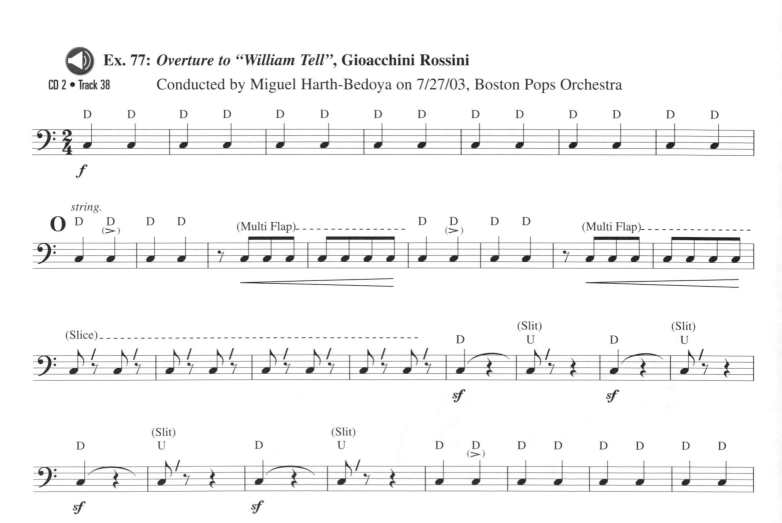

20. The Scissor

This stroke is really more of a sound effect and has limited use in the orchestral repertoire. Nevertheless, it may be used occasionally. To accomplish the **Scissor**, the cymbals are  placed together and kept against the chest throughout the stroke. The outside edges of the cymbals, away from the chest, are opened up momentarily, and a rhythmical sound is made by playing or slapping both cymbals together while they maintain contact with the chest. The sound is rhythmical and extremely dry with a maximum of contact sound and a minimum of cymbal ring. One may use the *Scissor* stroke successfully in works such as Leroy Anderson's "Blue Tango." Play four *Scissor* strokes in a row, then, on accented eighth notes on the "and" of beat 4, do a pseudo-*Single Flap* stroke, which is choked off harshly on the downbeat (thus producing a kind of short "choked" sound). Let the *Single Flap* stroke buzz a bit over the bar line, and then repeat as indicated throughout the entire piece.

Ex. 78: "Blue Tango," Leroy Anderson

CD 2 • Track 39   Conducted by Bruce Hangen on 5/27/00, Boston Pops Orchestra

Tempo di tango

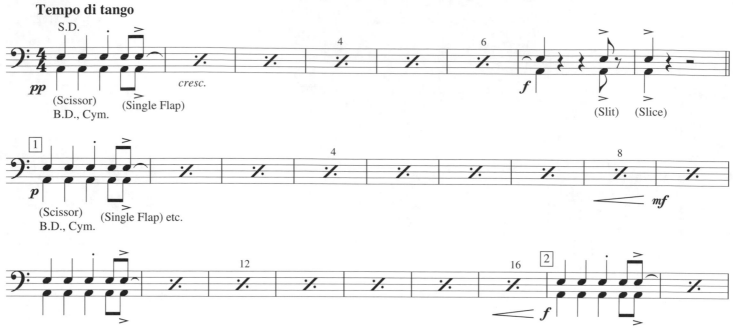

Edgard Varèse's *Amériques* written in 1921 and revised in 1927 is a half-hour long creative exploration that arguably predates every twentieth century sound and gesture known today. Its impact on both players and audience is not unlike Stravinsky's *Rite of Spring*. The work is difficult to play, with demands that are as extreme as its dynamics, from the softest to the loudest. Because of its technical demands and the number of players required—145 players in the original 1921 version—the work receives very few performances. This piece, like *Ionization*, another seminal work by the same composer, requires no less than thirteen percussionists.

The cymbal part in *Amériques* (Example 79) is unique in that it persists almost non-stop throughout the piece, from the softest sounds possible to some of the loudest. In this author's experience, there is no other piece that stretches a cymbal player's endurance as does this one. In fact, the piece incorporates some of the loudest and fastest playing ever encountered. For that reason alone it is challenging and fun to perform.

However, it is the opening of the piece that describes the primeval creation of the world in a most beguiling way. This is a master at work here without question. In two sections of the work the cymbalist is asked to play triplets on the off-beats, one measure after **9**. The tempo is such that in order to articulate the notes, the *Scissor* stroke comes into its own. A normal stroke here would just not articulate the passage succinctly. The *Scissor* stroke makes it happen. At number **17**, note the abrupt change of tempo in the middle of the passage. Once the *Scissor* stroke is in play, it is difficult to change tempo. Nevertheless, it is required, and so care must be taken that the repetitive motion is still flexible enough to accommodate this tempo change.

Ex. 79: *Amériques*, **Edgard Varèse**

CD 2 • Track 40

Conducted by James Levine on 8/17/05, Boston Symphony Orchestra

Note: on CD 2, track 40, there is a brief pause and new count-off before rehearsal number **17**.

21. The Shuffle

The Shuffle is a continuous and simultaneous movement

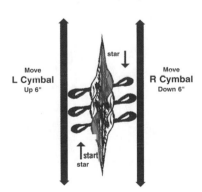

Yet another pops favorite, Anderson's "Bugler's Holiday," offers an excellent opportunity for the **Shuffle** stroke. The *Slit* stroke may be used for the first eight measures, followed by the *Shuffle*. This new stroke starts at rehearsal number **1** with cymbals starting as shown in the drawing and the photographs. It continues on the downbeats all the way through. The gesture of the *Shuffle* stroke is similar to climbing up a ladder. One cymbal reaches up, then the other cymbal reaches up. As one cymbal reaches up, the other slides lower. The cymbals

remain completely flat against each other and meet inround only in the middle of the stroke by sliding the top of the right cymbal over and down the top of the inside of the left cymbal, and vice-versa. While one cymbal is sliding down, the other one is sliding up. A kind of seesaw, floating stroke is produced. The sound that results is a smooth, continuous sound, with an outline of a downbeat audible throughout. Movement from high to low position is timed to fit the tempo and rhythm of the passage. Study the photos and the drawing.

Ex. 80: "Bugler's Holiday," Leroy Anderson

CD 2 • Track 41

Conducted by Robert Bernhardt on 6/8/96, Boston Pops Orchestra

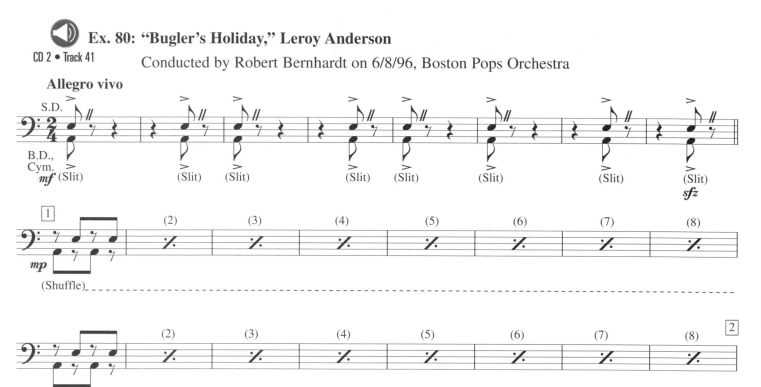

22. The Spin

The British composer Peter Maxwell Davies has come up with a new cymbal sound called a **Spin**. In his piece *An Orkney Wedding with Sunrise* (Example 81)—a work commissioned for the Boston Pops in 1985 and played many times since then—the composer labeled one of the newest cymbal sounds ever.

The *Spin* is best achieved by rotating a suspended cymbal, mounted on a hook, while gently resting one or two very thin triangle beaters on the edge of the cymbal. In order to give the cymbal some added momentum, wind the cymbal up (much like a clock) in the reverse of the direction that you intend it to spin. Then, with a gentle push, let it spin back while at the same moment gently placing two thin triangle beaters on the surface of the cymbal. The sound is both eerie and gentle, yet, because of the spinning cymbal, sustainable and audible for quite a long time. In the music, a gentle bass drum roll precedes the *Spin*. This is one of the great cymbal effects in the repertoire.

Ex. 81: *An Orkney Wedding with Sunrise*, **Peter Maxwell Davies**

CD 2 • Track 42

Conducted by Keith Lockhart on 7/9/96, Boston Pops Orchestra

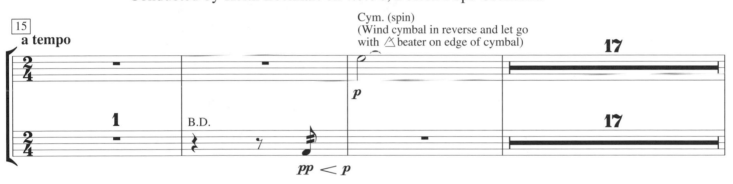

Chapter Six

CREATIVE INTERPRETATION
MAKES MATTERS MORE COMPLEX

The examples discussed so far have dealt with a number of special cymbal strokes, created to match a particular musical phrase, dynamic, and/or gesture. Orchestral cymbal performance might best be described as having two primary functions: to add a sense of color to the orchestration, and to help provide a solid rhythmic pulse. The examples given up to this point, however, have dealt almost exclusively with yet a third and far more subjective function: musical gesture. Next we will look at some examples in which cymbals play multiple roles, combining rhythm, color, and gesture all at the same time. Several pieces by nine different composers will be looked at.

PETER MAXWELL DAVIES

Peter Maxwell Davies, a remarkably creative composer, has another surprise for us. In this next example, the bass drum and cymbals are in an unusual "Ivesian" mode. Note the almost impossible rhythms required, especially of the cymbal player. There are no tricks here, just luck! However, the players should try to meet at the beginning of measure 238 so that the second and third beats are in place.

Ex. 82: *An Orkney Wedding with Sunrise*, **Peter Maxwell Davies**

Conducted by Keith Lockhart on 7/9/96, Boston Pops Orchestra

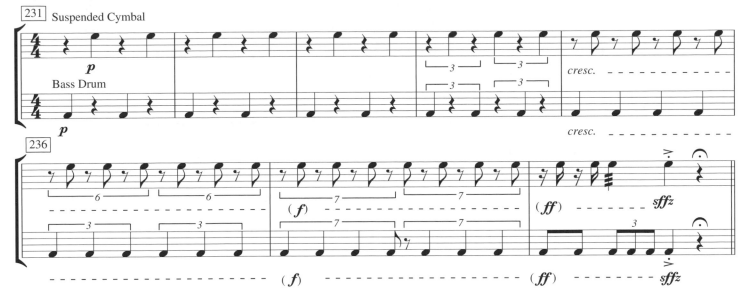

MAURICE RAVEL

Maurice Ravel's ballet score *Daphnis et Chloé* remains quintessentially the pre-eminent example of a virtuosic display of color and movement set in music. Two suspended cymbals are recommended: number one (1) is slightly higher in pitch and faster than cymbal number two (2), which is larger and more powerful. The next example shows the suspended cymbals entering at rehearsal number **197** with a dotted half note. In order to help accentuate rhythmic pulse and drive, the cymbal should be cut off exactly on the "and" of beat 3. This is repeated in the next measure. Then at the 2/4 measure, the half notes should be played as quarter notes, allowing a clean attack in both measures, and further supporting rhythmic drive and intensity. The four-measure *crescendo* that follows on cymbal (2) should begin slowly and peak at the last moment into **198**, where it ends with an *attacca*. At the very peak of the *crescendo*, while continuing to roll on the one suspended cymbal, strike a second suspended cymbal, thereby accentuating the *ff* at the downbeat of measure 198.

Ex. 83: *Daphnis et Chloé*, **Maurice Ravel**

Conducted by Frubeck de Burgos on 7/10/04, Boston Symphony Orchestra

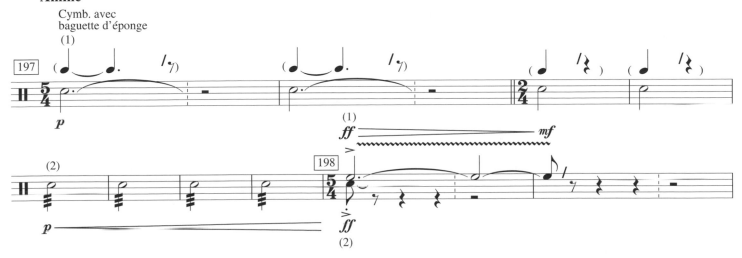

Example 84 shows the suspended cymbal playing a series of half notes. Actually, this section is one of the most driving, rhythmically propelled sections of the whole piece. In this series of 5/4 measures and 3/4 measures, the snare drum provides the rhythmic background and the cymbals add a splash of color. Continue to use two suspended cymbals here, beginning with the fast 17" splash cymbal for the half notes (note the edit in the music). These notes are struck with two mallets simultaneously to provide instant attack, and the notes are cut off a fraction before count 4 so as to again reinforce and accentuate rhythmic drive and intensity. In the following 3/4 measures, the half note is played like a quarter note followed by a quarter rest. Then, one measure before **202**, use the larger, more powerful suspended cymbal to provide additional thrust, for a fast and powerful *crescendo*. This is again cut off sharply just before the first count of the next two measures, permitting a clean attack on the following (edited) half note on count two.

Ex. 84: *Daphnis et Chloé*, **Maurice Ravel**

CD 2 • Track 45

Conducted by Frubeck de Burgos on 7/10/04, Boston Symphony Orchestra

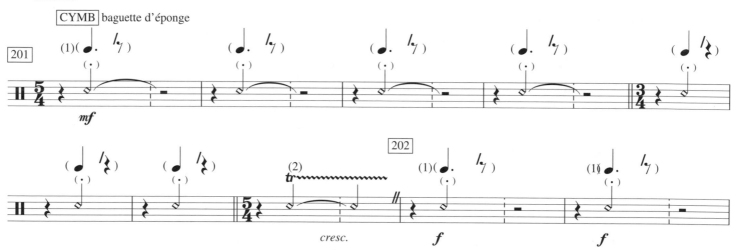

Example 85 offers additional good use of dual suspended cymbal play. Try to distinguish between quick eighth notes and thicker, fuller, and heavier quarter notes. The bass drum plays on counts 1, 3, and 5 at number **206**. A precise repetition of the bass drum part at **206** occurs in the cymbal part at number **207**, and the quality of that sound can be reiterated by playing precise quarter notes on the larger cymbal at the beginning of number **207**, immediately followed by a quick eighth note played on the smaller cymbal.

Ex. 85: *Daphnis et Chloé*, **Maurice Ravel**

CD 2 • Track 46

Conducted by Frubeck de Burgos on 7/10/04, Boston Symphony Orchestra

Exactly at the peak of the climax, Example 86, eight measures after **209**, the long *crescendo* roll can be topped off with an accented stroke on the second cymbal while continuing to roll on the first cymbal. Two measures later, while a general *decrescendo* is occurring, there is a quick *crescendo* and *decrescendo* played by the French horns, trumpets, and strings. While continuing to *decrescendo* on one cymbal, the cymbal player should also continue to accompany the brass and strings passage with two mallets in the left hand, first striking the cymbal crash as mentioned above, then playing a quick *crescendo* and *decrescendo* on the second cymbal.

Ex. 86: *Daphnis et Chloé*, **Maurice Ravel**

Conducted by Frubeck de Burgos on 7/10/04, Boston Symphony Orchestra

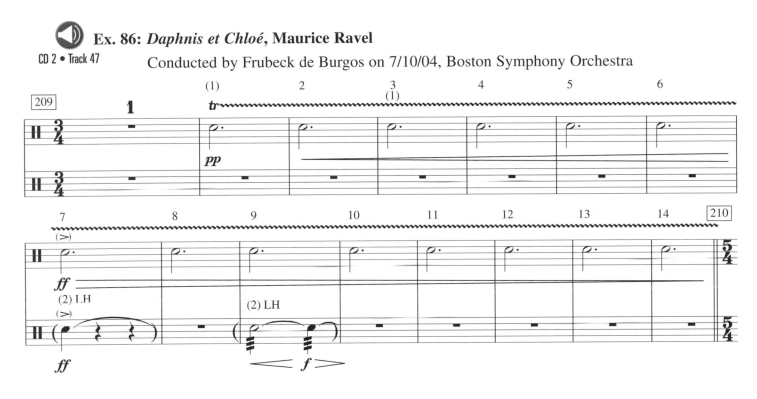

CLAUDE DEBUSSY

A similar opportunity presents itself in Debussy's *La Mer* where two suspended cymbals should be used. One small, fast cymbal is used for the soft strokes and soft *crescendo* measures. A larger, more powerful suspended cymbal is used for the loud strokes after rehearsal **32**.

Ex. 87: *La Mer, Mvt. 2*, **Claude Debussy**

Conducted by Robert Spano on 1/8/00, Boston Symphony Orchestra

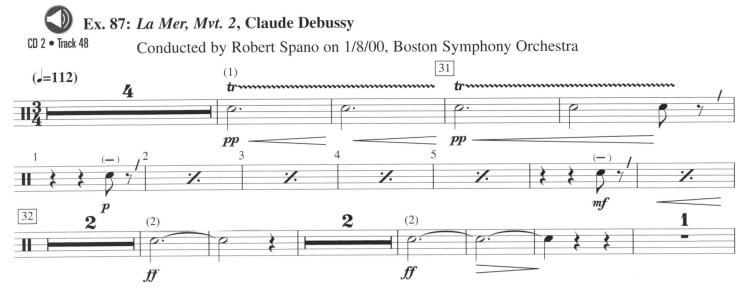

The concluding nine measures of the second movement bring us yet another performance problem: to make an extremely soft sound in such a way as to maintain good tone quality. These nine measures can be played in at least three different ways. The first is to strike a small, thin, fast, suspended cymbal in the normal manner. Another solution is to use a thin triangle beater and to simply scrape the cymbal with a gentle brushing motion from the center outward. A third way (and arguably, the most effective), is to use the *Whizz* or *Swish* stroke for all but the last of these notes, and a *Hiss* stroke for the last note of the piece. Some conductors will allow you a certain amount of freedom to experiment with this passage, while others will dictate how they want these notes played.

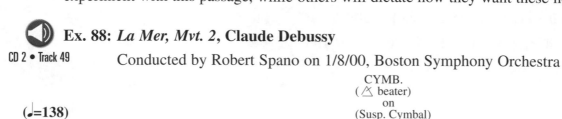

Ex. 88: *La Mer, Mvt. 2*, **Claude Debussy**

CD 2 • Track 49   Conducted by Robert Spano on 1/8/00, Boston Symphony Orchestra

Another unusual bit of writing occurs in the third movement. The next example was also discussed earlier as Example 13 on page 15. The grace notes here are unlike anything else in the cymbal repertoire, and they present a special problem for the performer. There are at least two ways to perform this. One way is to use crash cymbals to help bring out the notated flam by opening up and overtly accentuating a flam stroke. In this case, the notes three measures before **51** are immediately choked off after each flam. This is relatively easy to do with crash cymbals, yet difficult for the listener to hear. Use of a large suspended cymbal is preferred. With two very hard mallets in one hand, and by rolling the hand while striking the cymbal, make two distinct attacks while using the other hand to dampen the notes as they are played, and to muffle them completely immediately after.

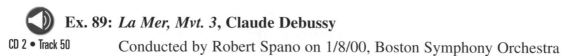

Ex. 89: *La Mer, Mvt. 3*, **Claude Debussy**

CD 2 • Track 50   Conducted by Robert Spano on 1/8/00, Boston Symphony Orchestra

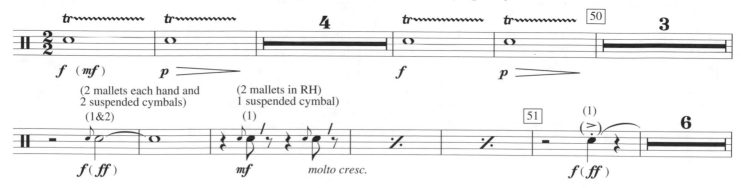

Beginning at **61** in Ex. 90, an effective choice is to use two 18" suspended cymbals simultaneously, repeating the same at two measures before **62**. Starting at the third measure of **63**, use the shaft of a plastic mallet, slapping the cymbal flat on, while choking the cymbal almost entirely with your other hand. This is a tricky passage to be sure, and is helped by a conductor who keeps the tempo absolutely steady until **63**. At **63** you should attempt to change back to regular suspended cymbal mallets to finish off the piece. The fourth measure from the end is played on one cymbal. For the last three measures, change over to a second cymbal. This allows for a nice clean accent at the beginning of the *ff* roll and another on the last downbeat of the piece.

Ex. 90: *La Mer, Mvt. 3,* **Claude Debussy**

CD 2 • Track 51   Conducted by Robert Spano on 1/8/00, Boston Symphony Orchestra

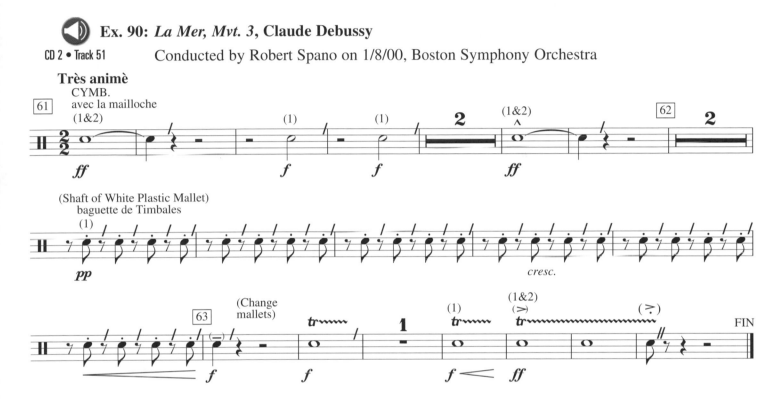

BÉLA BARTÓK

Undoubtedly one of the most unusual suspended cymbal parts is found in Bartók's Concerto No. 1 for Piano and Orchestra. This concerto—a work of almost demonic intensity in the two outer movements—features a sublime slow movement in which percussion and piano are singularly the most important agents. In this work, Bartók asks that the percussion be brought up to the front of the stage, near the piano to foster an unusual kind of intimacy, while acknowledging the soloistic nature of the percussion part! The slow movement is very similar in feeling and design to the slow movement of Bartók's Sonata for Two Pianos and Percussion. Here, however, the percussion writing is more developed and bold, and requires an unusual numerical system that is explained in the full-sized score, but *not* in the percussion part nor in the miniature score! Numbers **1** through **9** are employed over the notes, with numbers **3**, **4**, **5**, **6**, **7** and **9** relating exclusively to the suspended cymbal part, except that number 3 is an instruction for both the cymbal player and the snare drum player. These are instructions to indicate in the most precise way where and how to strike the suspended cymbal.

The percussion parts, or *batterie*, are written for tympani and three percussionists. Where two percussion parts are joined by a bracket ({), the two instruments concerned should be played by one performer. The triangle, bass drum, and tom-tom are to be played in the usual manner. All the percussion instruments, including tympani, are to be placed, if possible, directly behind the piano in front of the orchestra.

In this piece, Bartók has asked for four cymbals altogether as follows: two hanging cymbals, the other two to enable the *a dué* effect. The cymbal instruction *a dué* indicates that the two cymbals are to be played against one another.

The effect and manner of playing are explained by figures as follows:

1) In the center of the drumhead with tympani sticks

2) In the center of the drumhead with the tips of the side-drum sticks

3) Around the rim of the drumhead or the hanging cymbal with the tips of the side-drum sticks

4) Around the rim of the hanging cymbal with tympani sticks

5) Around the rim of the hanging cymbal with the butt-ends of the side-drum sticks

6) On the dome of the hanging cymbal with the butt ends of the side-drum sticks

7) On the rim of the hanging cymbal with the butt-end of one side-drum stick, while the other stick is fastened to the leather strap of the cymbal such that the tip of the stick touches the cymbal

8) With two side-drum sticks, commencing at the far rim of the side-drum, progressing gradually to the center of the drumhead, and then returning to the rim.

9) On the very edge of the cymbal with two tympani sticks.

This example shows the cymbal part with the unique number code over each note as well as what may be the most specific dynamic indications of any piece in the standard orchestral repertoire.

Ex. 91: Concerto No. 1 for Piano and Orchestra, Mvt. 2, Béla Bartók
Conducted by Simon Rattle on 9/10/93, Boston Symphony Orchestra,
Soloist: Peter Donohoe

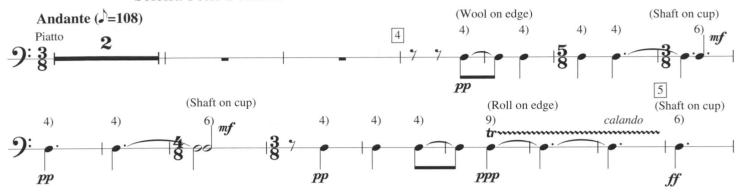

Example 92 shows more of the same, including three measures of the *Sizzle* cymbal effect in the eighth measure. Typically, a player would use a real sizzle cymbal here to good effect. Not many composers have gone to so much trouble to annotate such precise instructions.

Ex. 92: Concerto No. 1 for Piano and Orchestra, Mvt. 2, Béla Bartók
Conducted by Simon Rattle on 9/11/93, Boston Symphony Orchestra,
Soloist: Peter Donohoe

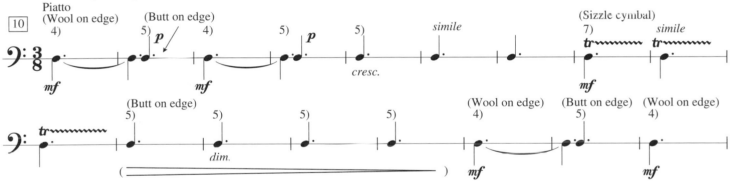

In Example 93 Bartók has written the part over two separate lines, clearly indicating what each hand is to play: right hand for the top score with snare-drum stick on the rim of the cymbal; left hand for the bottom score, with soft mallet on the rim of the cymbal. This is one piece where special effects are composed and clearly notated.

Ex. 93: Concerto No. 1 for Piano and Orchestra, Mvt. 2, Béla Bartók
Conducted by Simon Rattle on 9/12/93, Boston Symphony Orchestra
Soloist: Peter Donohoe

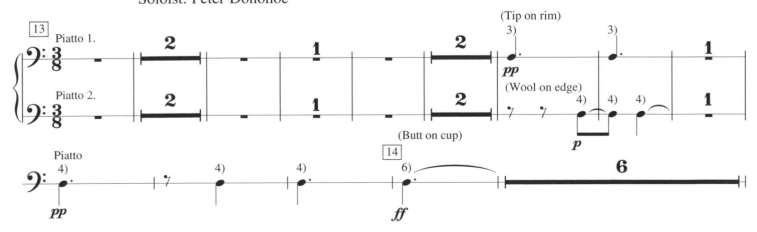

HECTOR BERLIOZ

Using Two Cymbal Players

Playing two notes in rapid succession on cymbals is at best an awkward proposition. The nature of the instrument is such that one wants to let the cymbals ring. In the next two examples, what would otherwise be an awkward situation may be circumvented by asking a colleague to help out. In Hector Berlioz's *Benvenuto Cellini Overture* (Example 94), at rehearsal number **6**, there is just such an opportunity. One player plays only the short sixteenth notes while the other player plays the half notes. This is a very satisfying solution and solves the problem very well. In fact, it feels quite good to play the long notes cleanly with a full stroke.

 Ex. 94: *Benvenuto Cellini Overture*, **Hector Berlioz**

CD 2 • Track 55 Conducted by Seiji Ozawa on 9/30/93, Boston Symphony Orchestra

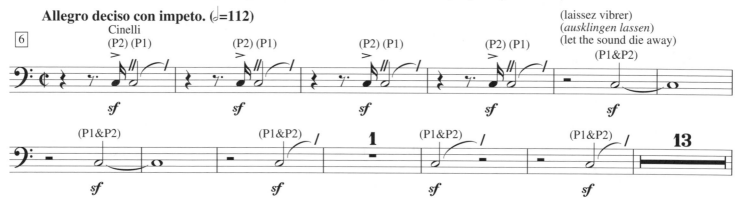

We continue this idea again at number **16** in Example 95, where one player plays the quarter notes and the other plays the half notes. This amplifies the wonderful syncopation that occurs in this section in a very natural way.

Ex. 95: *Benvenuto Cellini Overture*, **Hector Berlioz**

CD 2 • Track 56 Conducted by Seiji Ozawa on 9/30/93, Boston Symphony Orchestra

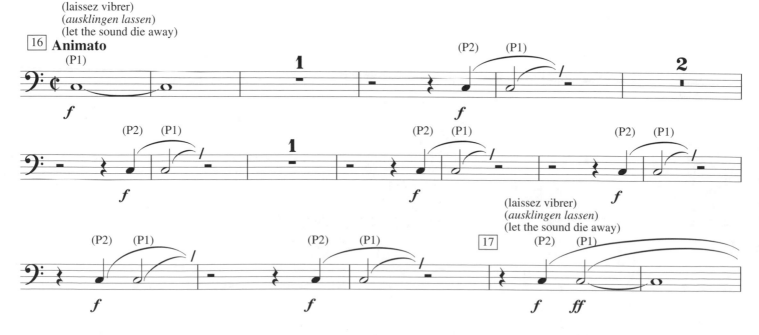

Finally, after number **19**, in Example 96, two cymbal players play again: one plays the quarter note before the bar line, and the other plays the quarter note on the following downbeat. Note the distinct suggestion for cutting off each note in all these passages.

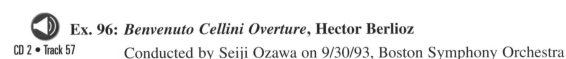

Ex. 96: *Benvenuto Cellini Overture*, **Hector Berlioz**

CD 2 • Track 57   Conducted by Seiji Ozawa on 9/30/93, Boston Symphony Orchestra

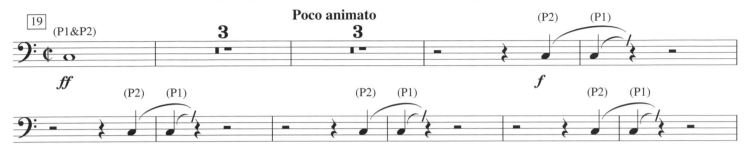

SERGEI RACHMANINOFF

A similar opportunity for dividing up a musical line between two players exists in Rachmaninoff's Symphony No. 2. Playing this part with two cymbal players makes this section come off far better. The extreme soft dynamics are easier to play with two cymbal players, and the rhythm and its syncopations swing more naturally with two players than if one player tried to play both notes.

Ex. 97: Symphony No. 2, Mvt. 2, Sergei Rachmaninoff

CD 2 • Track 58   Conducted by Andre Previn on 11/20/99, Boston Symphony Orchestra

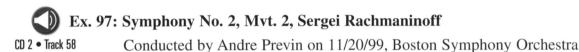

IGOR STRAVINSKY

Igor Stravinsky's *Petrouchka* offers the percussionist one of the most original bass drum-cymbal parts ever created. Just looking at it makes one realize and appreciate the genius behind this bit of creativity. The part is a marvel of ingenuity and is fun to play.

At the first entrance of the section, the single *mf* eighth note signals the activity that lies ahead. Dramatically the note should sound like a sneeze, short and comical, signaling the forthcoming activity. Prepare this note by setting your right hand (the one holding the bass drum mallet at the ready) at the height of the mounted cymbal, in order to be able to choke the sound immediately after it is made. The left hand holds a special small thin cymbal. It makes a quick scoop stroke into the body, so the top cymbal is immediately choked by the chest. Simultaneously, the bottom cymbal is choked by the right hand. As soon as the cymbal sounds are cut off, lower your right hand into playing position in preparation for the remainder of the passage. The excerpt must be played as evenly as possible allowing for a slight *decrescendo* in the last two measures, but without making a *ritard*. Finally, the last note played, just before **66**, should be muffled, allowing for a moment of complete silence for the most dramatic effect.

Stravinsky composed *Petrouchka* in 1911 and revised it in 1947. Interestingly enough, both versions remain in the repertoire. In playing this material it is crucial to know the melodic material that one is accompanying.

Ex. 98: *Petrouchka (1911 version)*, Igor Stravinsky

CD 2 • Track 59

Conducted by Charles Dutoit on 8/21/98, Boston Symphony Orchestra

Example 99 is the 1947 version of the same music as Example 98. The only real difference is the change in dynamics in the second measure from **mf** to **p**. The music looks different as the bass drum and cymbal notes are spaced more widely over the staff. Playing a subtle accent wherever the bass drum plays on the beat may be effective. Keep your knee on the drum to affect a slight muffle when playing the bass drum on the off-beats, and release the knee when playing on the beats. This creates a subtle *valse*-like feel beginning on the third beat of each measure starting at measure 125.

Ex. 99: *Petrouchka (1947 version)*, **Igor Stravinsky**

CD 2 • Track 60   Conducted by Charles Dutoit on 8/24/04, Boston Symphony Orchestra

Example 100 is the 1911 version of the *valse*. Once again it is important to clearly know and listen to the melodic line as one plays this music. This excerpt is in a quick *valse* tempo, conducted in one beat per measure, making the opening two measures difficult to execute. At the 2/4 measure, the notes slow down while the beat stays the same. Again, play a subtle accent whenever the bass drum plays on the downbeat, thus making a three-measure phrase.

 Ex. 100: *Petrouchka (1911 version)*, **Igor Stravinsky**

CD 2 • Track 61   Conducted by Charles Dutoit on 8/21/98, Boston Symphony Orchestra

Example 101 is the 1947 version of the same *valse*. Notice that three of the four opening measures have now been omitted, and just the duple-metered measures remain. The notation is clearer and simplified, thus easier to play.

Ex. 101: *Petrouchka (1947 version),* **Igor Stravinsky**

CD 2 • Track 62

Conducted by Charles Dutoit on 8/24/04, Boston Symphony Orchestra

SERGEI PROKOFIEV AND NICOLAI RIMSKY-KORSAKOV

O and +

In some cases composers do not tell you which cymbals they would like you to use, for example, crash cymbals or suspended cymbals. The music of Sergei Prokofiev and other Russian composers often omits any clear indication of which cymbals to use. Some of these composers employ a curious set of symbols (o and +) over the notes. No one to my knowledge has figured out precisely what these symbols mean. I have asked every Russian conductor I have come in contact with, and most of them just shake their heads and say, "I don't know."

One conductor however, Maestro Gennady Rozhdestvensky, answered me directly and without hesitation. He said that (o) means crash cymbals and that (+) means suspended cymbal. I have now accepted this as highly probable.

In practice I find that Mr. Rozhdestvensky's explanation actually supports what I have been doing in these situations for years. For example, I instinctively play most of Prokofiev's music on suspended cymbals, even if the part specifies otherwise because I feel ultimately that it sounds better. His Piano Concerto No. 3 (Example 102) comes most readily to mind.

Ex. 102: Piano Concerto No. 3, Mvt. 1, Sergei Prokofiev

CD 2 • Track 63

Conducted by James Conlon on 8/22/98, Boston Symphony Orchestra, Soloist: Garrick Ohlsson

In these situations, we as creative artists are left to consider, in purely musical terms, what the correct instrument should be. The musical gesture, the nature of the note (length and dynamic), or even technical issues, might lead one to prefer one instrument to another. Again, generally speaking, musical gestures that are *passive* (see Chapter One, page 3) in nature would lead one to use a suspended cymbal. Its horizontal position lends itself more to a coloristic effect that is passive in terms of more immediate directional energy.

The symbols (○) over the nine eighth notes in Rimsky-Korsakov's *Scheherazade* (Example 103) indicate the use of crash cymbals. If one were able to play the entire passage, including the fast sixteenth notes, on crash cymbals, the issue would be solved. However, this is not the case. The sixteenth notes are too fast to play with two crash cymbals and a struck suspended cymbal must be employed. One solution for performing this passage has already been explained in Example 26 on page 37.

Ex. 103: *Scheherazade*, **Nicolai Rimsky-Korsakov**

CD 2 • Track 64   Conducted by Seiji Ozawa on 4/7/93, Boston Symphony Orchestra

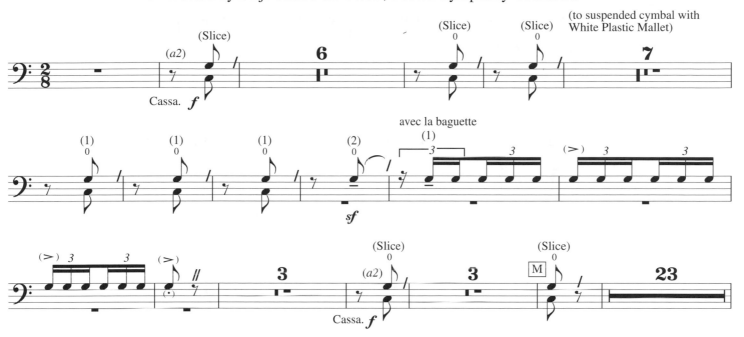

CLOSING REMARKS

As the reader has discerned by this time, playing the cymbals in an orchestra is a challenging endeavor. It is not just a matter of hitting the cymbals together at the right time, though initially that is a worthwhile goal. The following lists some of the important things one must do to becomes a successful cymbalist:

- Develop a variety of strokes and a variety of attacks.

- Develop an intimate knowledge and feel for the cymbals one has available, and know when to use them.

- Develop a number of strokes to articulate *legato*, *staccato*, and *marcato* attacks.

- Think "gesturally" by creating strokes and sounds that support the underlying musical gesture.

- Think creatively and experiment with a number of techniques to solve musical problems.

- Above all, think musically. The sound of the cymbals must *support* and *enhance* the musical moment. It must never interfere.

- Knowing when to play is crucial.

- Know when *not* to play. *When* to cut off the sound and *how* are equally important.

- Determining the exact role of the cymbals in any passage is essential.

- Determine whether notes are active or passive, rhythmic, coloristic or any combination of these. This will ascertain *how* one plays the passage, *with which* cymbal, *with which* mallet, *with what kind of* attack, and *with what kind of* follow-through.

- Determine the proper length of a note, and decide how to cut it off. Some notes are cut off aggressively while others are released to dissipate naturally. Decisions must be made for every entrance.

- Know your cymbals intimately. Know what they can and cannot do, especially with regard to pitch and dynamic control.

A cymbal technique must be developed which allows one to be creative. *Creative* technique is what this book is about, while it incorporates a step-by-step approach to learning how to play cymbals. Good technique allows one to play at any dynamic level with the ability to control and vary the moment of contact. A good technique, a musical mind, and a creative spirit will spur one on to articulate every musical moment in most unique ways.

Musical gestures, and portraying those gestures, are what make music and cymbal playing interesting. Included in this treatise is an entire chapter on special strokes or *Cymbalisms*, with examples of when and how to use them. These *Cymbalisms* can be used by anyone. However, one must be careful to use them discreetly. Because these special strokes are enjoyable to use, they are easily subject to abuse. Overuse, or use in the wrong context could interfere with the musical moment.

Many of these strokes should be of particular interest to marching band drum lines, since marching bands often employ several cymbal players at the same time. Doubling up on these techniques could open up many new exciting sounds and multi-layered effects. The effect of utilizing six cymbal players in the Berlioz *Requiem* supports this notion. In fact, any of the *Cymbalisms* used in this fashion will be unusual and dramatic, all the more so when performed by multiple cymbal players. Utilizing more than one of the strokes simultaneously and/or alternating different strokes in sequence will have yet another effect. In short, utilizing *Cymbalisms* will add special interest to any percussion section. The added colors available could easily be used in a cymbal cadenza-type section and should spark a whole new interest in cymbal performance.

In compiling the excerpts used in this book, I have found pieces that are not often talked about. I have described cymbal parts that are not necessarily included in the standard repertoire. In trying out the specialized techniques, one should become acquainted with this broader and more comprehensive repertoire. The techniques employed obviously can be utilized in the standard repertoire as well. Whatever music one plays, complementing and enhancing the musical moment are what remain most important.

—Frank Epstein

Appendix I
ORCHESTRAL CYMBAL LITERATURE

Composer	Title	Ex. No.	Page	CD Track
Anderson, Leroy	*Blue Tango [opening]*	78	78	39, CD 2
	Bugler's Holiday [opening]	80	80	41, CD 2
Bartók, Béla	*The Miraculous Mandarin [101]*	61	64	22, CD 2
	The Miraculous Mandarin [59]	63	66	24, CD 2
	The Miraculous Mandarin [36]	64	67	25, CD 2
	Concerto No. 1 for Piano and Orchestra. Mvt. 2 [4]	91	89	52, CD 2
	Concerto No. 1 for Piano and Orchestra. Mvt. 2 [10]	92	89	53, CD 2
	Concerto No. 1 for Piano and Orchestra. Mvt. 2 [13]	93	89	54, CD 2
Beethoven, Ludwig van	*Symphony No. 3, "Eroica," Mvt. 2. [mm. 236-241]*	49	54	10, CD 2
Berlioz, Hector	*Requiem [81]*	42	48	3, CD 2
	Benvenuto Cellini Overture [6]	94	90	55, CD 2
	Benvenuto Cellini Overture [16]	95	90	56, CD 2
	Benvenuto Cellini Overture [19]	96	91	57, CD 2
Bizet, Georges	*Carmen Suite No. 1, No. 5, Les Toreadors [A]*	16	29	16, CD 1
Britten, Benjamin	*Concerto No. 1 for Violin and Orchestra, Mvt. 3 [47]*	58	62	19, CD 2
	War Requiem [89]	59	62	20, CD 2
	Concerto No. 1 for Violin and Orchestra, Mvt. 1 [opening]	66	68	27, CD 2
	Concerto No. 1 for Violin and Orchestra, Mvt. 1 [10]	67	68	28, CD 2
Bruch, Max	*Scottish Fantasy [opening]*	65	67	26, CD 2
Chabrier, Emmanuel	*España [O]*	12	14	12, CD 1
Davies, Peter Maxwell	*An Orkney Wedding with Sunrise [15]*	81	81	42, CD 2
	An Orkney Wedding with Sunrise [231]	82	83	43, CD 2

Composer	Title	Ex. No.	Page	CD Track
Debussy, Claude	*La Mer, Mvt. 2 [42]*	2	4	2, CD 1
	La Mer, Mvt. 3 [43]	6	10	6, CD 1
	La Mer, Mvt. 1 [14]	9	11	9, CD 1
	La Mer, Mvt. 3 [61]	10	11	10, CD 1
	La Mer, Mvt. 3 [50]	13	15	13, CD 1
	Fétes, from Nocturnes [22]	44	49	5, CD 2
	La Mer, Mvt. 3 [48]	52	58	13, CD 2
	La Mer, Mvt. 2 [31]	87	85	48, CD 2
	La Mer, Mvt. 2 [42]	88	86	49, CD 2
	La Mer, Mvt. 3 [50]	89	86	50, CD 2
	La Mer, Mvt. 3 [61]	90	87	50, CD 2
Dvořák, Antonín	*Symphony No. 9, Mvt. 4 [2]*	47	52	8, CD 2
	Otello Overture [21]	60	63	21, CD 2
Kodály, Zoltán	*Háry János Suite, Mvt. 4 [1]*	62	65	23, CD 2
Mahler, Gustav	*Symphony No. 1, Mvt. 4 [1]*	7	10	7, CD 1
	Symphony No. 1, Mvts. 3 and 4 [16]	29	39	29, CD 1
	Symphony No. 2, Mvt. 5 [10]	43	49	4, CD 2
	Symphony No. 9, Mvt. 3 [36]	70	69	31, CD 2
Moussorgsky, Modeste	*Pictures at an Exhibition, V. Ballet of the Unhatched Chicks [48]*	5	9	5, CD 1
	Pictures at an Exhibition, V. Ballet of the Unhatched Chicks [48]	74	72	35, CD 2
	Pictures at an Exhibition, V. Ballet of the Unhatched Chicks [55]	75	73	36, CD 2
	Pictures at an Exhibition, VII Limoges– The Market [65]	76	74	37, CD 2
Nestico, Sammy	*Good Swing Wenceslas*	46	52	7, CD 2
Prokofiev, Sergei	*Romeo and Juliet, Second Suite [1. Andante]*	8	11	8, CD 1
	Scythian Suite [3]	11	12	11, CD 1
	Piano Concerto No. 3. Mvt. 1 [21]	102	96	63, CD 2

Composer	Title	Ex. No.	Page	CD Track
Rachmaninoff, Sergei	*Piano Concerto No. 2, Mvt. 3 [32]*	28	38	28, CD 1
	Symphony No. 2, Mvt. 2 [35]	97	91	58, CD 2
Ravel, Maurice	*Daphnis et Chloé [194 Animé]*	1	2	1, CD 1
	Bolero	14	15	14, CD 1
	La Valse [17]	17	30	17, CD 1
	Alborada del Gracioso [3]	31	41	31, CD 1
	Alborada del Gracioso [16]	32	41	32, CD 1
	Alborada del Gracioso [9]	33	41	33, CD 1
	Alborada del Gracioso [14]	34	42	34, CD 1
	Alborada del Gracioso [28]	35	42	35, CD 1
	Alborada del Gracioso [34]	36	43	36, CD 1
	Valses Nobles et Sentimentales, IV [27]	54	60	15, CD 2
	La Valse [45]	69	69	30, CD 2
	Daphnis et Chloé [197 Animé]	83	83	44, CD 2
	Daphnis et Chloé [201 Animé]	84	84	45, CD 2
	Daphnis et Chloé [205 Animé]	85	84	46, CD 2
	Daphnis et Chloé [209 Animé]	86	85	47, CD 2
Rimsky-Korsakov, Nicolai	*Scheherazade [L] (same as Ex. 72)*	26	37	26, CD 1
	Scheherazade, Allegro molto e frenetico	71	70	32, CD 2
	Scheherazade [R]	72	71	33, CD 2
	Scheherazade [L]	103	97	64, CD 2
Rossini, Gioacchini	*Overture to "William Tell" [O]*	77	76	38, CD 2
Sibelius, Jean	*Finlandia [N]*	27	38	27, CD 1
Sousa, John Philip	*The Stars and Stripes Forever*	39	45	39, CD 1
Strauss, Richard	*Don Juan [Cc]*	3	5	3, CD 1
	Ein Heldenleben [14]	40	47	1, CD 2
	Ein Heldenleben [19]	41	47	2, CD 2
	Don Quixote [27]	50	55	11, CD 2
	Don Quixote [12]	55	60	16, CD 2
	Don Quixote [17]	56	61	17, CD 2
	Don Quixote [conclusion]	57	61	18, CD 2

Composer	Title	Ex. No.	Page	CD Track
Stravinsky, Igor	*Petrouchka (1947 version) [124]*	4	9	4, CD 1
	Firebird	30	40	30, CD 1
	Petrouchka (1947 version) [93]	51	56	12, CD 2
	Petrouchka (1947 version) [74]	73	72	34, CD 2
	Petrouchka (1911 version) [65]	98	92	59, CD 2
	Petrouchka (1947 version) [124]	99	93	60, CD 2
	Petrouchka (1911 version) [73]	100	94	61, CD 2
	Petrouchka (1947 version) [144]	101	95	62, CD 2
Suppé, Franz von	*Light Cavalry Overture [Maestoso]*	37	44	37, CD 1
	Light Cavalry Overture [C Allegro brilliante]	38	44	38, CD 1
Tschaikowsky, Peter I.	*Symphony No. 4, Mvt. 4 [1]*	15	28	15, CD 1
	Symphony No. 4, Mvt. 4 [13]	18	31	18, CD 1
	Symphony No. 4, Mvt. 4 [13]	19	32	19, CD 1
	Symphony No. 4, Mvt. 4 [13]	20	33	20, CD 1
	Romeo and Juliet Overture [E]	21	34	21, CD 1
	Romeo and Juliet Overture [T]	22	34	22, CD 1
	1812 Overture	23	35	23, CD 1
	Capriccio Italien [P]	24	35	24, CD 1
	Swan Lake, No. 5, Danse Hongroise, Czardas [47]	25	36	25, CD 1
	Symphony No. 6, Mvt. 4 [mm. 134-146]	48	53	9, CD 2
Varèse, Edgard	*Amériques*	79	79	40, CD 2
Vaughan Williams, Ralph	*A Sea Symphony, Mvt. 4 [Aa]*	53	59	14, CD 2
Wagner, Richard	*Götterdämmerung, Act 3 [59]*	45	50	6, CD 2
	Siegfried's Rhein Journey [36]	68	69	29, CD 2

Appendix II
TWENTY-TWO CYMBALISMS

	Composer	Title	Page	CD Track
1. Zischend	Strauss, R.	*Ein Heldenleben*	47	1, CD 2
		Ein Heldenleben	47	2, CD 2
	Berlioz	*Requiem*	48	3, CD 2
2. Hiss	Mahler	*Symphony No. 2, Mvt. 5*	49	4, CD 2
	Debussy	*Fêtes, from Nocturnes*	49	5, CD 2
3. Swish	Wagner	*Götterdämmerung, Act 3*	50	6, CD 2
4. Swirl	Nestico (arr.)	*Good Swing Wenceslas*	52	7, CD 2
5. Frizzle	Dvořák	*Symphony No. 9, Mvt. 4*	52	8, CD 2
	Strauss, R.	*Don Quixote*	55	11, CD 2
6. Frizz	Stravinsky	*Petrouchka (1947 version)*	56	12, CD 2
7. Grizzle	Debussy	*La Mer, Mvt. 3*	58	13, CD 2
8. Grizz	Bartók	*The Miraculous Mandarin*	64	22, CD 2
9. Whizz	Vaughan Williams	*A Sea Symphony, Mvt. 4*	59	14, CD 2
	Ravel	*Valses Nobles et Sentimentales, IV*	60	15, CD 2
	Strauss	*Don Quixote*	60	16, CD 2
	Britten	*Concerto No. 1 for Violin and Orchestra, Mvt. 3*	61	19, CD 2
		War Requiem	62	20, CD 2
10. Prezz 1	Dvořák	*Otello Overture*	63	21, CD 2
11. Prezz 2	Bartók	*The Miraculous Mandarin*	64	22, CD 2

	Composer	Title	Page	CD Track
12. Roll	Kodály	*Háry János Suite, Mvt. 4*	65	23, CD 2
	Bartók	*The Miraculous Mandarin*	66	24, CD 2
13. Crusher	Bartók	*The Miraculous Mandarin*	67	25, CD 2
14. Sizzle	Bruch	*Scottish Fantasy*	67	26, CD 2
	Britten	*Concerto No. 1 for Violin and Orchestra, Mvt. 1*	68	27, CD 2 28, CD 2
15. Kiss	Wagner	*Siegfried's Rhein Journey*	69	29, CD 2
	Ravel	*La Valse*	69	30, CD 2
	Mahler	*Symphony No. 9, Mvt. 3*	69	31, CD 2
16. Slice	Rimsky-Korsakov	*Scheherazade*	70	32, CD 2 33, CD 2
	Stravinsky	*Petrouchka (1947 version)*	72	34, CD 2
	Moussorgsky/Ravel	*Pictures at an Exhibition, VII. Limoges– The Market*	74	37, CD 2
17. Slit	Moussorgsky/Ravel	*Pictures at an Exhibition, V. Ballet of the Unhatched Chicks*	72-73	35, CD 2 36, CD 2
18. Single-flap	Bruch	*Scottish Fantasy*	67	26, CD 2
19. Multi-flap	Rossini	*Overture to "William Tell"*	76-77	38, CD 2
20. Scissor	Anderson	*Blue Tango*	78	39, CD 2
	Varèse	*Amériques*	79	40, CD 2
21. Shuffle	Anderson	*Bugler's Holiday*	80	41, CD 2
22. Spin	Davies	*An Orkney Wedding with Sunrise*	81	42, CD 2